END PAPERS

THE BOOK-COLLECTOR MASQUERADING AS
MASTER OF HOUNDS

An imaginary portrait by H. J. Brothers

END PAPERS

Literary Recreations

By

A. EDWARD NEWTON

KENNIKAT PRESS/PORT WASHINGTON, N. Y.

END PAPERS

Copyright 1931, 1933 by A. Edward Newton
Reissued in 1969 by Kennikat Press
Library of Congress Catalog Card No: 75-86574
SBN 8046-0578-5

Manufactured by Taylor Publishing Company   Dallas, Texas

ESSAY AND GENERAL LITERATURE INDEX REPRINT SERIES

Respectfully dedicated to

AGNES REPPLIER AND CAROLINE SINKLER

*who in their several capacities lend
distinction to this so-called
City of Brotherly Love*

CONTENTS

CONTENTS

ILLUSTRATIONS

"In submitting to the public eye the following collection, I have not only to combat the difficulties that writers usually encounter but may incur the charge of presumption for obtruding myself on the world, when, without doubt, I might be, at my age, more usefully employed." — BYRON

―――――――

"Digressions, incontestably, are the sunshine; — they are the life, the soul of reading! — take them out of this book, for instance, — you might as well take the book along with them; — one cold eternal winter would reign in every page." — STERNE

The author wishes to express his thanks to the following editors, publishers, and individuals for permission to reprint portions of the material in this volume: to the editors of the *Saturday Review of Literature*, the *Atlantic Monthly*, the *Yale Review*, the *Colophon;* to Houghton Mifflin Company, Columbia University Press, the Limited Editions Club; and in particular to Miss Carolyn Wells, Mr. William M. Elkins, and Mr. Hugh Tregaskis.

END PAPERS

LAWYERS WERE CHILDREN ONCE

CONSIDERING what "an everyday young man"
I am, it is really surprising how many and
what pleasant things happen to me; perhaps it
is because I am always ready to meet an agree-
able situation a little more than halfway.

Some time ago I was dining in London when
a man opposite me at a table remarked, "I knew
I should meet you sometime; I want to thank
you for a pleasant review you once wrote of a
book of mine." Now, as I almost never write
a book review, I replied that I was afraid I did
not deserve his good opinion, and went on to
inquire what the book was. *The Old Benchers
of the Inner Temple*, he told me, and then I
remembered that several years before the
Saturday Review had sent me a book which had
so pleased me that I wrote a half a column or
so of praise, sent it off, and dismissed the matter
entirely from my mind.

"I am glad," said my friend, who turned out to be Sir Frank Mackinnon (himself an Old Bencher), "to meet a fellow Lamb enthusiast. Some day when you have time . . ." "In London I have nothing but time," I interrupted. "Go into the Temple Gardens," he continued, "and stand with your back right against the wall of Number 2 Crown Office Row, then turn around and look right above your head, and you will see a tablet which I have caused to be erected there; I think you will approve of it. Here is a card" (handing me one) "which will open any gate and most doors in the Temple. After you have noted the inscription, turn again and look towards the river, and far down across the lawn you will see a little bronze figure of a boy which you may think of as Charles Lamb: he is looking towards Crown Office Row, 'the place of his kindly engendure.' Particularly notice the book he has in his hand, upon the open page of which you will see a quotation from Lamb's essay on 'The Benchers' which you quoted with excellent effect in your paper, 'Lawyers were children once.'"

There is before me as I write a well-thumbed

and badly shaken little volume, *The Essays of Elia and Eliana*, which I have owned for more than half a century and which I always turn to when I want to verify a quotation. Truth compels me to say that the original manuscript of Lamb's exquisite essay, "Dream-Children," is a more valuable possession, but it was in this little volume, published by Moxon, that I first learned to know and love the author "who wrote for antiquity," he said, and who, as Mr. E. V. Lucas remarked, "has become more and more a writer treasured by posterity."

And this may be as good a place as any to insist publicly upon the merit, the exceeding merit, of Lucas's *Life of Charles Lamb*. I am not without experience. With Dr. Johnson I can exclaim, "Sir, the biographical part of literature is what I love most." I have read many biographies, and, Boswell excepted (one excepts Boswell from force of habit, almost), I have no hesitation in saying that Lucas's *Lamb* is the masterpiece. It has gone into ten editions — there should have been fifty.

May I now reprint the review of *The Old Benchers* as it originally appeared and won for

5

me a new-old friend with whom I have since prowled the streets and courts of his (and my) beloved London?

This is a lovely book. Charles Lamb is always appealing; but how pleased and amazed and amused he would be to think of the great Oxford University Press making into a beautiful and substantial volume his little paper on "The Old Benchers of the Inner Temple," where, as he says, he was born and passed the first seven years of his life.

The best essays are always autobiographical, — the creator of the essay, old Montaigne, taught us that, — and Charles Lamb's most delightful papers are those in which he refers to his own experiences: the names of dozens of them spring to our lips. But in essay writing, as Dr. Johnson said of a man writing an epitaph, one is not under oath: the essayist may take a thread of truth and string thereon a pearl — many pearls — of fiction. And commentators are frequently misled thereby. I have been told that Lamb's "Oxford in Vacation" was written not after a visit to Oxford but after a visit to

6

Cambridge. The story fits one place quite as well as another. Lamb made love to several shadowy maidens in his essays that may never have lived at all, and we know — what his contemporaries did not — that he loved and proposed to and was declined by Miss Kelly, "she of the divine plain face."

And so we who love the choicest cuts of Lamb have always taken his "Benchers" with a grain of salt. Did they all live in the flesh and did Lamb see them clearly or only in his mind's eye? These questions and many another Sir Frank Mackinnon has answered for us, and given us little biographies and reproductions of many portraits which make us wish we were a Bencher. I might perhaps be mistaken for a wise man did I wear a wig and a robe: many men are so mistaken.

How fully saturated with London Charles Lamb is, and it with him! Only a few weeks since, one moonlight night, I spent an hour wandering in the Temple thinking of the realities and the shadows which once had habitation there, and of the Shakespeare story of the white rose and the red, and of Tom Pinch and his sister and

7

John Westlock. Can the fountain which Charles Lamb "made to rise and fall" many times be the one into which I threw a penny not long ago, as one does in the Trevi fountain at Rome? Hardly — but one fountain is as good as another if one be not thirsty, and it suggests pleasant memories.

How felicitous is Lamb in a phrase! Example: "Lawyers, I suppose, were children once."

How wonderful his selection of the right word! Example: "What a dead thing is a clock with its *embowelments* of lead!"

But Lamb is in danger of being somewhat overdone. Thackeray called him a "saint"; that was silly: let me not say another word, but this — to end where I began: *The Benchers* is a lovely book.

But delightful essay as "The Benchers" is, and many others are, none have the whimsical, emotional, and tender charm of "Dream-Children." Never before, at least not since the Elizabethans, has the English language been spun into finer fabric than in this essay, especially the last paragraph. Its writing gave Lamb some concern: it is the only paragraph he had occasion to blot. It was written in Lamb's golden year, and the original manuscript of this essay is the golden crown of my Lamb collection, which is not a mean one.

I obtained the original from Dr. Rosenbach many years ago, on the day when the Germans sank the *Lusitania*. Everything else, including our hearts, sank in consequence. It was hardly a day for successful book-hunting, but Harry B. Smith's *Sentimental Library* had just been put on sale, and one felt that one must rise to the occasion.

In the delightful catalogue that he made of his books and manuscripts and letters, he refers to "Dream-Children" as the most expensive item he ever bought — no, I am mistaken, he so refers to it in his book, *First Nights and First Editions*, and wonders what has become of it. Let this brief paper tell him.

The essay was written on a large sheet of India House paper.

Holding the original against a strong light, one may see that the first title was not "Dream-Children" but "My Children." Then Lamb, with unerring taste, realized that a bachelor should only have "Dream-Children," and changed the title of his essay accordingly.

Everyone writing on Charles Lamb has joined in the symphony of praise which this paper has evoked. Canon Ainger, once Master of the Temple, says: "Inexpressively touching, when we have learned to penetrate the thin disguise in which he clothes them, are the hoarded memories, the tender regrets, which Lamb, writing by his lonely hearth, thus ventured to commit to the uncertain sympathies of the great public." Charles Dickens calls it "the most delightful paper, the most charming essay which the tender imagination of Charles Lamb ever conceived; it represents him sitting by his fireside on a winter night, telling stories to his own dear children, delighting in their society, until he suddenly comes to his old, solitary bachelor self, and finds that they were dream children who might have been but never were." E. V. Lucas calls "Dream-Children" "the most beautiful of all his writings," and again, as though loath to leave the subject, he refers to it as "that beautiful tissue of wistful regrets and delicate im-

DREAM CHILDREN
After a drawing by C. E. Brock

aginings." And C. T. Winchester, in a little book of critical essays, has this: —

Only once or twice — perhaps only once, in that most intimate of all his essays, the "Dream-Children" — does Lamb drop all affectations and tell us the things that lay nearest his heart in language too utterly sincere even for the disguise of his "self-pleasing quaintness." In that perfect essay humor is quite lost in pathos; and the English in which the simple story is told, for purity of idiom, chaste simplicity, and artless grace of movement, is quite unsurpassed. No one else in Lamb's day wrote such English, and to find anything so perfect you will have to go back to the best passages of the English Bible. Here Lamb has set up a glass where we may see the inmost part of him.

The essay was originally printed in the *London Magazine* for January 1822, and appeared in book form the following year in the famous *Elia* series, in two volumes. Glancing at the table of contents of the first volume, we see the board "in richest commonalty spread": "The South Sea House," "Oxford in Vacation," "Grace before Meat," "Poor Relations," "Mrs. Battle," and many more. To read the titles is like hearing the music of a well-known hymn. The words come to one. "A clear fire, a clean hearth and the rigor of the game. . . . Old Sarah Battle (now with God)." "The Old Benchers of the Inner Temple" — and this brings me back to my "Old Bencher," Sir Frank Mackinnon, not yet with God.

II

ON FORMING A LIBRARY

EVERY collector has, I suppose, received requests to show his collection to some person or persons who think they are interested, but who, in fact, merely want to say, "Oh, yes, I know Mr. Blank and his collection very well." Now if one is lucky enough to have collected paintings or prints, or indeed anything that will display itself, it is easy enough to say, "Come when you like," and on the arrival of one's guests turn them loose. But with books which must be shown and explained, it is a very different matter. This is what I mean. There is a little volume of *Poems by Currer, Ellis and Acton Bell* (actually the three Brontë sisters) : a copy with the Aylott and Jones imprint may be worth five or six hundred pounds, while the same book with a Smith, Elder imprint is no great bargain at ten.

A "collector" of English poetry hardly needs to be told the sad history of this slender volume :

how, one day, Charlotte Brontë found a blank book filled with verses in the handwriting of Emily, and how after much discussion and some correspondence the three sisters — for Anne wrote, also — decided upon the publication of a small volume which should contain verses by all of them. But no publisher cared for the venture, until finally Messrs. Aylott and Jones, of London, agreed to publish upon the payment by them of thirty-odd pounds. The girls agreed, and after some delay the volume appeared. A year later the publishers reported the sale of just *two* copies. The disappointment of the sisters may be imagined, but they took the blow philosophically and, each giving away a copy or two, decided to send the remaining sheets to the trunk makers; but finally, having received an offer from Smith, Elder and Company, they transferred the sheets to them, and in due course to the public. Hence it is that a copy of the book with the Aylott and Jones imprint is rare. There is, too, some further question as to binding, some copies having a lyre stamped in blind upon the side, others a geometrical design; which has priority? My friend Morris L. Parrish

says that there are at least four different
bindings and that the geometrical is the earliest :
that is one matter settled. Some such explanation as this has to be made about pretty much
every book one shows to one's visitor if he is to
carry away with him any proper idea of what
a collection of rare books really is. One can
make such an explanation once, or even ten
times, with a certain amount of enthusiasm —
after that it becomes a task.

I once had this experience. I found a man
rubbing his dirty hands over a fine copy of
Blake's *Songs of Innocence* and assuring another
that *it must be lithographed because it was colored!*
My first thought was to kill this man, but,
realizing that he might be dear to someone, I let
him live. Relating this experience to a friend
in London, he told me how he dealt with such
situations. My friend has a famous collection
of modern poetry : Wordsworth, Shelley, Byron,
Keats, Tennyson, Browning, and the rest — all
in excellent original bindings. When strangers
descend upon him he does not show his rare
books, but something which pleases his visitors
quite as well. Taking a small key from his

pocket and pointing to a case over in a corner, he says something like this: "You know poetry is my strong point; here is the key to that bookcase yonder: be very careful, but enjoy my books to your heart's content." Then when he sees a book tumble to the floor, or the rector set a teacup on a book instead of in a saucer, he never turns a hair, for all the books in that case have been picked up at odd times and places for about sixpence each, invariably lacking the "points" which would make them valuable; they might, indeed, be called lightning rods designed to protect first editions from destruction. By this little chicane all parties are pleased: Mr. Blank has "shown his books" and Mr. Splash and Miss Dash have seen them.

But I have had other experiences. Some time ago, Professor Spiller of Swarthmore College brought to my home a company of young men and maidens who were "taking English" under his direction, and I was struck with their keenness and intelligence; one of them, a mere slip of a girl, stood me up and put me through an oral examination on Boswell's *Life of Johnson* from which it was difficult for me to escape with credit. So when, quite recently, that same Spiller asked if he might bring a small group to see my books, I wrote him that I would take on ten or a dozen students on any afternoon that would be convenient to all parties. In due course my guests arrived; some entered my library shyly, some inquiringly, some keen upon seeing a first edition of some particular book which they had been studying under Professor Spiller's guidance. And here let me digress long enough to say that if I were a teacher of English literature I should try to instill into pupils the idea that literature is a reflex of life, and endeavor to make it as interesting as life itself. It is a terrible thing to let a student get the idea into his head that some great world-rocking book is "required" reading. And if I were asked how this is to be done, I should say treat every great book as though it were a great man: in the words of Walt Whitman, —

> Camerado! this is no book,
> Who touches this touches a man.

But however much of a man a book may be to-day, it was, once, almost certainly a child; its birth may have occasioned its parent an amount of anguish which the mother who bore you never knew. Great books have to struggle for existence; for every book that survives, a thousand — ten thousand fall. It is worth while, then, to examine the survivor carefully and to discover why it has withstood the changes and chances of this wicked world.

But to return to my visitors. There was, I fancy, a certain amount of shyness at first, but it soon passed off; then someone asked a question, and before it was fully answered another was asked, and almost before we knew it the ice was broken and we all began to have a good time. I never met a more intelligent lot of boys and girls; one lad instantly challenged my attention by asking if I had a first *Lyrical Ballads*. To ask such a question is to start something, for this is perhaps the most significant, interesting, and tricky volume of poetry in our literary history, and presently I was engaged in telling my interrogator the story of the first issue of this book, which is indeed not unlike that of the Brontë sisters, except that in due course it was seen that *Lyrical Ballads* marked a turning point in English poetry. And I went on to say that when the first issue was brought out by Biggs and Cottle at Bristol, in 1798, its sale was but little larger than the first issue of the Brontë Poems, and that the book, for the copyright of which Cottle had paid Wordsworth thirty guineas, was also in peril of the trunk maker, when he decided to ship the book, in "quires," up to London, where it appeared under the patronage of J. and A. Arch, and very gradually the book made its way. All this took place in 1798. The first poem in the little volume was the "Rime of the Ancyent Marinere," no mention being made of the fact that it was by Coleridge.

Two years later another *Lyrical Ballads*, in *two* volumes, with Wordsworth's name on the title-page, appeared, with a long and elaborate preface in which the author developed his idea of what poetry is and should be. A quick sale is usually synonymous with an early death; a slow, halting sale, like a flickering flame never quite going out but always looking as though it would, may presage a conflagration. But the *Lyrical Ballads*, in two volumes, we now know contains some of the finest poetry ever written. At length comes the bibliophile, the collector, and says to himself, or out loud: "I must have a *Lyrical Ballads* with the Bristol imprint." How many are there? I don't know. Mr. T. J. Wise, of London, whose word is law, tells me he knows of six. I once, many years ago, had a copy offered me for seven hundred and fifty dollars, but I could n't see it — the seven hundred and fifty dollars, that is. Mrs. Cynthia Morgan St. John did, however; and her entire Wordsworth collection, probably the finest in the country, was later given to Cornell University by Victor Emanuel. Swinburne calls it the Black Tulip of English Literature. What is a copy worth to-day? Who shall say? Five or ten thousand dollars, perhaps: they are unobtainable. A copy with the London imprint is worth five hundred dollars at present and is pointed to ten times the figure. My copy, bound, but uncut, with the errata and the two pages of advertisements, was once dear at five pounds.

All this may be dull going to the reader, but to a student who is reading seriously it is a great delight to hold in his hands the cluster of little volumes which once made such a stir in the world before the theories which they expounded had gained acceptance. While I was endeavoring to make this, or something like this, clear, I could see a girl who was eagerly awaiting a pause to break in with a question: had I a copy of Blake's *Poetical Sketches*, and was it not published earlier and did he not anticipate Wordsworth in his breaking with the school of Pope? "Yes to all your questions," was the reply. Here is the *Poetical Sketches*, 1783; but Blake was a shooting star whose light went out. Wordsworth founded a school: his influence continues right down to the present. Matthew Arnold, who is only now taking his proper place as a poet, was especially influenced by him. Yes, I think Arnold's sonnet to Shakespeare very fine: I don't know that it shows the influence of Wordsworth especially, but it is magnificent: —

> Others abide our question. Thou art free.
> We ask and ask: Thou smilest and art still,
> Out-topping knowledge. . . .

It was written when Arnold was a very young man; the original manuscript I read a few weeks ago in the British Museum. Yes, it is almost an impertinence to praise Shakespeare. Yes, I have visited Nether Stowey, and a more sordid, miserable town I have seldom seen. Coleridge does not interest me much: I was early set against him by an essay in Augustine Birrell's *Obiter Dicta*. Let me read you a bit out of the volume I bought in 1885 and have read many times since: —

"Lamb, speaking of his sister Mary, who, as everyone knows, throughout 'Elia' is called his Cousin Bridget, says: 'It has been the lot of my cousin, oftener, perhaps, than I could have wished, to have had for her associates and mine freethinkers, leaders and disciples of novel philosophies and systems, but she neither wrangles with nor accepts their opinions.' Nor did her brother. He lived his life cracking his little jokes and reading his great folios, neither wrangling with nor accepting the opinions of the friends he loved to see around him. To a contemporary stranger it might well have appeared as if his life were a frivolous and useless one as compared with those of these philosophers and thinkers. *They* discussed their great schemes and affected to probe deep mysteries, and were

22

constantly asking, 'What is Truth?' *He* sipped his glass, shuffled his cards, and was content with the humbler inquiry, 'What are Trumps?' But to us, looking back upon that little group, and knowing what we now do about each member of it, no such mistake is possible. To us it is plain beyond all question that, judged by whatever standard of excellence it is possible for any reasonable human being to take, Lamb stands head and shoulders a better man than any of them. No need to stop to compare him with Godwin, or Hazlitt, or Lloyd; let us boldly put him in the scales with one whose fame is in all the churches — with Samuel Taylor Coleridge, 'logician, metaphysician, bard.'"

There is something more, but it ends with: "There are some men whom to abuse is pleasant. Coleridge is not one of them. How gladly we would love the author of 'Christabel' if we could! But the thing is flatly impossible. His was an unlovely character. . . . In early manhood Coleridge planned a Pantisocracy where all the virtues were to thrive. Lamb did something far more difficult: he played cribbage every night with his imbecile father, whose con-

23

stant stream of querulous talk and fault-finding might well have goaded a far stronger man into practising and justifying neglect. . . . Coleridge married. Lamb, at the bidding of duty, remained single, wedding himself to the sad fortune of his father and sister. Shall we pity him? No; he had his reward — the surpassing reward that is only within the power of literature to bestow. It was Lamb, and not Coleridge, who wrote 'Dream-Children: A Reverie.'"

This is a long quotation, but it served to introduce one of my most valued possessions: the original manuscript of "Dream-Children." It was written on India House paper, when Charles Lamb should have been busying himself with the price of ivory and indigo and such matters. "Yes, I think the last paragraph of 'Dream-Children' ties with Sterne's recording-angel paragraph in *Tristram Shandy* as the finest bit of prose in the language, and I feel sure that Professor Winchester, that admirable critic, would have agreed with me."

"*Tristram Shandy?* Yes, and a great book it is. First edition, in nine volumes, in red levant, over there."

Then I went on to say that I little thought, almost fifty years ago, that one day I should call Augustine Birrell a personal friend. Yes, I know him very well: I gave him a luncheon at the Garrick Club the last time I was in London. He is a crusty old bookman, but I hope some day to be a crusty old bookman myself. I had a letter from him only a few days ago, in which, speaking of Dickens, he said, "My love for him burns as brightly as ever." Bless his heart. Birrell is now in his eighty-fourth year and is a good deal of a prisoner in his home in Chelsea. He is a fellow trustee of the Johnson House in Gough Square, and used to be one of the best after-dinner speakers in London, full of grit, wisdom, and wit, with the grit first.

"My Johnsons are over there under the portrait, quite a row of 'em. . . . No, I do not pretend to understand Blake's *Prophetic Books* and I mistrust the man who says he does. . . . *Moby Dick!* Now you are talking! I have the English edition in three volumes, which was published in London in 1851, and the New York edition published the same year, in one. It is said that the three-volume edition is shorter than the one-volume edition. It would be interesting to compare the differences between the two texts and discover what, if anything, is omitted. But *Moby Dick*, any edition, English or American, is not one book but two: there is the book which you may read at a glance, and a book written between the lines, as it were, a book as psychical and as mystical as if it had been written by Swedenborg, whose disciple, in a sense, its author surely was. Melville was a genius and, like most great geniuses, was neglected in his lifetime. He was only a little more than thirty years of age when he wrote the book by which he will always be remembered. With its publication he practically ceased to exist, for, while he lived in New York until 1891, he did nothing important — his candle went out, but not until he had illuminated with it the paths of countless other men. Everyone who has written of the sea since Herman Melville's time is indebted to him. . . . My *Pickwick Papers* — I have two: one too good to show and one just good enough. . . . *Paradise Lost* — yes, in the safe in the other room — a *Comus* too. . . . No, I have no Bunyan's *Pilgrim's Prog-*

ress; it's a very rare book. Yes, Dr. Rosenbach has one, and my friend Sir Leicester Harmsworth has two. . . . Yes, I have a First Folio of Shakespeare. My ambition has been to get a copy of the first issue of every great, superlatively great book in English literature. No, I have not achieved it; who does? And my progress is now very slow. Understand rightly the terms which we are using. Gray's *Elegy* is a great poem, but not excessively rare. Congreve's *Incognita* is excessively rare, but not great. . . . My favorite novelist? Dickens, in spots; but for steady reading, Trollope. My favorite novel? Well, that depends on the weather. Yes, I love Jane Austen."

And so it went on for several hours, one question after another, light and heavy, until I happened to notice that Spiller was regarding my mental acrobatics with some amusement; whereupon I said to him, "You can afford to smile. You are highly paid (hear! hear!) for answering such questions; I'm doing it for fun. How on earth did you arouse in these young people such an interest in books?"

And then he let me into the secret: now comes

the pith of this paper. It appears that several years ago a gentleman, now dead, conceived the idea of giving to Swarthmore College a small sum of money — fifty dollars, I think it was — each year, to be awarded as a prize to the student, man or woman, who during his or her term at college formed the best collection of books. It was not, originally, thought to be a matter of much importance, and the rules laid down for the selection of the winner were not too rigid. Then someone in authority appointed a committee to make the award. Unfortunately, at the death of the originator of the scheme it was found that no provision had been made for carrying on the idea, and it was feared that the present year would be the last in which the prize would be awarded. Immediately it struck me that here was a way in which I might do much good with little money, as Benjamin Franklin often did. He once wrote a friend: "I am not rich enough to afford *much* in good works, and so am obliged to be cunning and to make the most of a little." The more I thought of this Swarthmore idea, as I called it, the more it appealed to me. How Franklin would have rejoiced at the idea of perpetually making a book-lover or several book-lovers for so small a sum as fifty dollars! So I then and there told Spiller that I was prepared to carry on the plan, taking care that the scheme should not lapse at my death. President Aydelotte was made acquainted with my offer, accepted it, and the deed was done.

The idea of making the award permanent seemed to make it advisable to formulate a set of rules. With these I wished to have nothing to do, for I am, personally, an unruly fellow. It seemed, however, necessary to consider some standards to which those entering the competition might be referred, and the following ideas were suggested by those having the matter in charge.

That an award of fifty dollars should be made annually to the student who, during an agreed-upon term, had

(*a*) Formed the best, not the largest, collection of books in one or more departments in which the student was specializing, be it literature, chemistry, engineering, or what not.

(*b*) Given evidence by the selection and care of his books of his appreciation of the joy of ownership. It was recognized that few, if any, students can, while at college, afford the luxury of first editions, but well-edited editions printed by responsible publishers are always to be preferred to showy books made to sell rather than to be read.

(*c*) Could pass reasonably well an oral examination upon his library and who knew why the edition he had selected was to be preferred to some other.

The idea can be made of great and lasting benefit and delight to those who in the formative years learn the joy of having a collection of books of one's own. And there is no college so poor as not to have a man, or group of men, who will bind themselves to give every year fifty or a hundred dollars for the purpose indicated; and the scheme can be developed indefinitely. God forbid that I should say a word against a public library, but nothing will take the place of a rack or a shelf full of books by one's own chair, close to a well-adjusted light, whether it be a lamp or a window. Everyone's shelf will contain different books, and the books which give joy to youth

JIMMY HATLO VISUALIZES THE AUTHOR OF "THIS
BOOK-COLLECTING GAME"

may not delight age, but the pleasure of reading continues. The habit, firmly established, enables one to endure, if need be, misfortune and even disgrace. I see to-day greater anxiety written on the faces of my millionaire friends than I do on the faces of the poor men who resort day after day to our public libraries, there to solace themselves with a book. In an established love of reading there is a policy of insurance guaranteeing certain happiness till death.

The afternoon was drawing to a close: I was tired, but my visitors were inexhaustible. I asked someone — I have forgotten who — to send me an essay he had written on the subject of the award, which subsequently I read with pleasure and with increased belief in the plan. I deeply regret that it is not original with me; it is something to be able to pass it on. I agreed to visit Swarthmore and make the next award; I did so, and had no difficulty, out of sixteen entries, in selecting the best. It was the "library" of William H. Cleveland, the young fellow who had questioned me upon Wordsworth's *Lyrical Ballads*. If he had any first or scarce editions I did not see them. There were no sets, but a better-selected lot of books — poetry, essays, fiction, and biography, a hundred or so — I never saw. In many of the books a special index of ideas rather than of names had been made on the blank leaves at the end, supplemented with a few extra sheets. I myself make such notes when reading, but my lists are always in a mess and are largely unintelligible, whereas Cleveland's indexes were alphabetically arranged and neatness itself.

In these days it is not necessary for a man to spend much money upon the purchase of a representative collection of books. While it is a pleasant thing to have many and fine books, it is by no means necessary, for, as Voltaire said, "it is with books as with men — a very small number play a very great part." The great publishing houses vie with one another in bringing out "libraries" of books which have the merit of being clearly printed, on good paper, well bound, and of a size which may be easily held in the hand and carried in one's pocket. What could be better, and cheaper, than the volumes in the Everyman's Library of Messrs. Dent, or the

World's Classics issued by the Oxford University Press, to mention only two out of the many "libraries" which have very largely taken the place of the old "Bohn books" which were popular when I was a lad. Carlyle suggests, somewhere, that the main use of college training is to teach one to read, "the true university being a collection of books." A hundred great books, or half that many, may well supply one with the intellectual stimulation, and recreation, of a lifetime. We have been told that no man is a hypocrite in his pleasures; quite so, and a man may so train himself that his pleasure may be had from reading the best books. I know whereof I speak.

It would be a pleasant thing to compile a list of one hundred great books which nobody reads to-day. This is not to suggest that they are useless; it means simply that they have done their work, that they have been "chewed and digested," in Bacon's phrase, and have unconsciously become a part of us, and we, without our knowing it, have become a part of them. Lewis Hind, a few years ago, published a book in London in which he showed that by the expenditure of only twelve pounds one could buy one hundred of the world's best books. His list would not be my list, nor would my list be his, but almost any list is a good list provided it is selected honestly.

Shortly after my experience with my young college friends, I sat next to an important New York publisher at dinner and I talked to him about the Swarthmore scheme, as I called it. He was strong for it, wanted me to write a little book about it which he said he would publish, but I wanted a wider spreading of the idea. It is for that reason that this paper first appeared in the *Atlantic Monthly*. That a publisher would be taken with the idea is not remarkable; the number of book-buyers would be increased by the general acceptance of the scheme. Publishers have to think of sales, but I am not a publisher; I am thinking only of the pleasure with which a man in after years will point to the collection of books made when a student at college. "Those books," he might say, "established in me the love of reading, and the love of reading has been the joy and solace of my life."

And so this paper is, in a way, an advertisement, — an advertisement of an idea, — and any skillful advertising man will tell you that, provided the idea is good, it is just as easy to advertise an idea as it is to advertise a hat or a pair of shoes. And the thoughtful reader is asked to answer — to himself — whether the idea of which I have told is good or no. I repeat that it is not mine: I am — to use a modern phrase — merely selling it. I hope I have advertised a good idea neatly. In any event, Swarthmore College is committed to it, and that, in the minds of the judicious, is a guarantee of its excellence.

III

MARY WEBB

It is well when one makes a prophecy to make a good one, without reservations; it is in this frame of mind that I sit down to write a few words upon a woman whose name will, I believe, fill the speaking trump of future fame as surely as — well, mine will not. Mary Webb is my subject. She is undoubtedly one of the greatest women writers in English literature. She was born at Leighton, a hamlet in the west of England, on the twenty-fifth of March, 1881. Christened Gladys Mary, — her father's name was Meredith, — she was called Glad. Meredith by her friends. At twenty she was almost a confirmed invalid; at thirty she married, and at forty-six she had put on immortality — not as one does in the fifteenth chapter of First Corinthians, but as one does when one has created several works of art. Her death passed practically unnoticed in the papers; even to-day, seven years after the event, her name is not given in that invaluably up-to-date book of reference, *Everyman's Encyclopædia*.

I am not quite sure how I stumbled across Mary Webb or her books, but opening, recently, a first edition of one of her novels, I came across a long letter from my friend Greville Worthington; at the time it was written — it has no date — he was a member of the bookselling firm of Elkin Mathews, 33 Conduit Street. I regret that Worthington has deserted a distinguished business and "gone into the City," as they say in London. I give his letter without permission, addition, or deletion: —

You have touched me on a spot in which I am most tender — Mary Webb. Ever since I began to read her, and I have read everything she wrote, I have thought her a most remarkable writer. For sheer beauty of country description she is very hard to beat. There is no doubt that she was, during her life, a much neglected genius. I do not think she was unhappy because I am sure that she must have been quite self-sufficient, and so it was perhaps better that she should have been neglected. The isolation from which she suffered (both physical — because she was a little stunted person with, I have heard, a horrible goitre — and moral) must have had much to do with that beauty of sadness of which you very rightly speak.

I am sending you an article which I happened by chance to notice in this month's *London Mercury*, and which is very good. As a matter of fact, I think the only writer to whom she can be compared is Emily Brontë.

I could go on for a long time about Mary Webb. She has caused me more pangs of realization of sudden perfect beauty than almost any other writer, certainly any modern writer.

Now — her first editions. I have only seen one copy of *Precious Bane* in my life and that I sold here in this shop for seven and sixpence before I had read it. I have never seen another and I have never regretted an action like that one. I have all her other first editions myself: they are very scarce. You see she was a difficult person to deal with and no publisher would deal with her twice. Every book was published by a different firm and every one was a failure.

Edgar Wells, in New York, had a brand-new copy of *Gone to Earth* when I was in America and I should buy it if I were you. I think it was thirty dollars. We cannot get her books over here.

I think her first novel, *The Golden Arrow*, is her best. Baldwin discovered her through William Bridgeman (now Lord Bridgeman) who was in his cabinet and lived in Shropshire. Mary Webb and her husband had a stall in Shrewsbury Market and used to sell garden produce. It all seems so incredible now, but as I say if there was ever a neglected genius it was she.

I am very pleased you have justified the opinion I have so long held about her and I hope you 'll tell everyone else.

Well, there you are. I sent at once to Edgar Wells in New York and secured his copy of *Gone to Earth*. Then by dint of much letter writing and long searching I secured her other books: *The Golden Arrow, The House in Dormer Forest, Seven for a Secret*, and *Precious Bane*, which last authorities regard as her best book. My own choice is *Gone to Earth*. Her volume of poems and essays, which has for title *Poems and the Spring of Joy*, I still lack. It was not published until after her death.

Adequately to describe the entrancing beauty of Mary Webb's prose would require the genius of Mary Webb herself; I shall not attempt it. Her stories cannot be read rapidly, nor can they be skipped. She has more than a touch of Thomas Hardy at his best, say, in *Under the Greenwood Tree*, yet she is in no sense an imitator. She could not help but write; one feels that even without Thomas Hardy we should have had the

Shropshire Lass. Her tales are all tragic; even the most unresponsive of us is moved, almost to tears: I am, and I am a hard-headed old fellow whose tear ducts dried up in infancy.

She was entirely neglected during her lifetime. The *London Times Literary Supplement* — which sets the critical pace in London, and which always reminds me of the critic in *Fanny's First Play* who must be told the author's name before he can tell whether the play is good or no — could find little to say for Mary Webb, as it could find little good to say of Holbrook Jackson's *Anatomy of Bibliomania* when it discovered that its learned author was not of either of the Universities. It was indeed quite by chance, as Worthington says in his letter, that in the year of her death one of Mr. Stanley Baldwin's secretaries — Mr. Baldwin was Prime Minister at the time — handed him, just as he was leaving Downing Street, a book to read on the train. "It's a Shropshire story; you'll like it, I think." The book was *Precious Bane*, which had then been published eighteen months. When Mr. Baldwin returned from his journey he wrote the author an enthusiastic letter with his own hand. What a gentlemanly act!

Mary Webb, by now married to a man as poor as herself, was greatly affected by the war. Her husband was a school-teacher; they were very poor, and the increased cost of living made it necessary for them to give up a tiny cottage, which cost only thirty-six pounds a year, for a smaller one, the cost of which was only thirteen! It was in this cottage that *The Golden Arrow* was written, in three weeks — a sufficient task for a woman in robust health; what must it have been for an invalid? Coaching pupils in a remote hamlet in war time was a precarious business, and her husband fell ill. It then occurred to Mary that she might add a few shillings to their income by the sale of flowers in Shrewsbury Market, nine miles away. *She walked this distance, getting up at three o'clock in the morning to pick her roses in order that they might be fresh when she reached her stall in the market. And after she had disposed of her stock she had a nine-mile walk home.* I know nothing in all literary history more touching than this.

Yet she kept on writing, and slowly, very

slowly, she found her public: it was a very select one. Then it was suggested that she go to London to be near publishers and physicians. She was not easy to deal with. They took a house in Hampstead, not much more than twice the width of the front door, near the Underground Railway Station. Here she wrote book reviews and did other literary chores, but her health became worse, and they moved again; they were always moving. It may well be that the Stanley Baldwin letter gave her the thrill of her life; her letter in reply would suggest this. And then she died, of Graves' disease, on October 8, 1927, and her body was taken to Shrewsbury for burial. A few months later, at a Royal Literary Fund Dinner, Mr. Baldwin made a speech in which he said he was happy that he had sent her a few words of appreciation in time. And Sir James Barrie referred to her "as the best of our writers, yet no one buys her books." They do now. She has a good publisher in London, Jonathan Cape, and another in New York, E. P. Dutton & Company. Her husband, who survives, must be in receipt of large royalties. How ironical it all seems.

MARY WEBB

When I sent the prospectus of this volume to the most modest and sympathetic of editors, Ellery Sedgwick, I was lucky enough to call forth this response: —

My dear Newton: —

The table of contents of *End Papers* tickles my imagination, and my mind rests particularly on one — Mary Webb. What do you know of her? For many years there was a genuine intimacy between us in London, but I was baffled by the enormous difficulty of adapting her peculiar genius to the people's taste. One of her papers I did publish, and I cannot tell you how many I read. And then one day she begged me to come and see her. I journeyed to Hampstead, and shall never forget that afternoon. In her pinched and hungry little flat, she had spread her tea table with buns which I well knew had made inroads into her last shilling, and which choked me as I ate them. The door was partly ajar, so that she might hear her sick husband when he called her from his bed. Such a good man as he was, she told me, gallant and enduring, but with about the capacity of an unweaned baby when it came to making headway against the world. They had married in spite of poverty, and she had had enormous pleasure through him until tuberculosis killed their hopes. It seems he had a submastership in a Board School, and earned, as I remember, 180 pounds a year. She herself was worn to the bone, and into it, I think, for she had not long to live.

43

When I left her, I went on to Galsworthy's, and told him that a woman of very great talent was dying almost of starvation a mile away. We talked the Civil List, etc., etc., and then the next day, which was my last day in London, I went to see Bennett, and told him something simply must be done.

When I got on the steamer, there were in my bag three of her stories, and I well remember reading them in bitterness of spirit, because it was only too obvious that they could only flourish in a selective audience such as I had not to offer them.

Six months after I came back she died, and then came the extraordinary incident of the Prime Minister. I think it was my old friend, John Buchan, who gave him the book. The incident has always been on my conscience. I must have bungled somewhere, for certainly I was nearer her by far than any other editor.

From a book-collector's point of view, Mary Webb in first editions is difficult, almost impossible. Her books were published at a bad time; everything was bad — printing, paper, cloth binding, everything. The editions were small, and the books fell to pieces in the reading. There are no "points" — at least I know of none; variations in color of binding mean nothing except that, owing to the war, binders used what cloth they had.

As I complete this little story, an English

bookseller's catalogue reaches my desk. It quotes three of Mary Webb's books. Under *The House in Dormer Forest* is this note: "Mary Webb is unquestionably one of the great women writers in English literature, and with Katherine Mansfield can claim equality with any accepted classics of the past. No modern could be more attractive to the collector; her books total only six, — counting in a volume of nature studies, — are completely free from the idiotic 'rarities' abounding in many modern bibliographies, all genuinely rare and of real importance. I cannot stress too strongly the difficulty of obtaining her books. Since reading *Precious Bane* three years ago I have searched consistently, and during that period I have only seen or heard of (apart from mine) four copies of *Precious Bane*, none of *Gone to Earth*, and one each of the others. I allude, of course, to good copies. Compare such a record with the flood of *Jane Eyres*, *Tom Joneses*, second Shakespeares, *Vicars of Wakefield*, and Boswell's *Johnson!* These are not rare — they are only expensive."

Under *The Golden Arrow* is this: "Two copies of Mary Webb's first book; a most interesting item presenting two binding variants, but which of the two can claim priority I cannot say. As far as I know, no bibliography of Mary Webb has been compiled. Probably both were issued simultaneously, a possible explanation being that, due to the war, binders had not sufficient cloth of one color to complete the edition."

And *Gone to Earth:* "A magnificent copy in the original dust wrapper, wrapper slightly defective." Then the bookseller goes on to say: "I believe this to be Mary Webb's rarest book; produced in the worst period of the war with the shoddiest of materials, copies in even presentable condition seem to be as mythical as the Dodo. Any 1917 printed dust wrapper is a rarity."

I know nothing of the relative scarcity of Mary Webb's novels, but this I believe to be her best. It has not, I think, its superior in English fiction. It was my intention to say something more of this story, but I should only defeat my own end — that of giving pleasure to my reader. Suffice to say that it is the most beautiful and tragic story I know. I think I shall never hunt the fox again. "Gone to Earth! Gone to Earth!"

IV

NOW IT MAY BE TOLD

ON November 21, 1930, there died in Philadelphia a man who had been identified with the retail book business for more than sixty years. Need I say that I refer to Edwin B. Campion — Ned Campion, as he was familiarly called by his many friends. I had returned from Europe only a day or two before, and, having occasion to call Dr. Rosenbach on the telephone, I was told by Mr. Lawler that he would be in in half an hour, that he was attending Mr. Campion's funeral. "Don't tell me Ned Campion is dead!" I cried. "Why, the last time I saw him he told me he was going to live forever!" "Well, he came pretty near doing it," was the reply. "Where is the funeral?" I asked; was told, looked at my watch, hung up the receiver, seized a hat and coat, jumped into a taxi, and was just in time to pay my respects to the memory of a man I had known intimately for well over half a century. In recent years I had not seen much of him: we had with the passage of time drifted apart, as old friends will, almost unconsciously. It is a brief story of an experience I had with Ned Campion some three years ago that is the subject of this paper.

I received one day in my office a letter from my old friend which gave me pause and at the same time made me smile. Campion wanted to know when it would be convenient for me to have him call on me, that he wished me to do him a favor. I felt a touch in that letter. Ned was most scrupulous in money matters. I had never lent him a dollar in my life, but somehow I thought the time had come when I would, and said to myself, "I will not lend him the thousand dollars he will certainly wish to borrow. I should never see a penny of it again. But for old time's sake I shall give him two hundred and fifty — that much I will do with pleasure; I may even make it five hundred." I then called him on the phone and told him that my office was on the top floor of a big factory building; that he was sure not to find the elevator, and that it would kill him to climb the stairs. "I'll call on you," I said, "to-morrow at about noon." Perhaps he would take lunch with me.

Next morning, providing myself with a blank check, to be filled in as emergencies dictated, I presented myself at Ned Campion's shop. He was in excellent spirits, as he always was, and told me a good story. My old friend prided himself rather upon his impudence: in this I acknowledge myself his disciple. He had, too, a wit, a humor, that was all his own. I told, several years ago, in the *World's Work*, a story of his once waiting on an old Quaker lady in Porter & Coates's bookstore, which for the time and for Philadelphia was at least as important as Scribner's or Dutton's, in New York, is to-day. I was employed in the store, but I was not supposed to have sufficient intelligence to sell books. My sponsors thought that in time I might be taught how to dispose of pens, ink, and paper — how much fun I have with them now! How well I remember thinking, "Some day I shall be permitted to sell books," but the time never came.

Porter & Coates was a Quaker concern, and

was patronized by men and women who wore the Quaker garb and employed the plain language. The competition of the department stores was terrific, and it was the firm's silly idea to meet this competition and crush it. One day a stout old lady came in to buy a novel: "she did not know what she wanted, she wanted to look around." Finally she fell into the clutches of Ned Campion, at that time a dapper young man.

"A novel, madam? Yes, madam. Have you read *Ben-Hur?*" — at that time the book of the year. The lady had not — "did not care for the title."

"It's an excellent book, madam. I assure you. Yes, perfectly proper. One dollar and ten cents."

Here I must digress to say that the retail price of this excellent novel, published by Harper & Brothers, was one dollar and a half. The trade discount for small quantities was a "third off"; on larger orders, a "third and five"; and on good big orders, "forty." It was the habit of the bookstores to bunch their orders so as to get the maximum discount, which made the cost of the book ninety cents. Overhead and profit were to come out of the tiny sum of twenty cents. It was a ridiculous situation: one could make a better living selling papers in the street.

"That is the cut price, madam; the regular price is one dollar and a half. . . .

"Have I a rubbed copy? No, madam, but *I shall be glad to rub this one for you.* Yes, madam, one dollar ten is the lowest price. . . .

"Another color binding? No, madam, they are all bound in the same color. That is the latest shade — *elephant's breath.* . . .

"Do we deliver? Certainly. . . .

"No, madam, not to-day; early to-morrow — it would cost ten cents carfare and take a boy over an hour to go and come from West Philadelphia. . . .

"Friend in a hospital? Sorry! Doubtless will remain until to-morrow. I'm sorry we can't deliver it before to-morrow. Charge it? Certainly. What name?" And all this to make twenty cents.

Another story, and then to my narrative. Ned Campion was, one summer's day, riding in a street car in Philadelphia. In those days it was customary for men to wear pearl-gray derby hats; we all did — none of those soft, flabby things we wear now. Well, Campion had taken his hat off and put it on the seat beside him; the seats then ran along on either side of the car. He was intent with his newspaper, or perhaps he was making eyes at a pretty girl across the aisle (I have known him to do such things); at all events, he did not notice a Quaker lady of magnificent beam enter and, without looking where she was sitting, plump herself down upon his hat, which instantly became a ruin. Gradually raising herself therefrom, she handed him that which a moment before had been a fine Dunlap hat. "I fear I have sat upon thy hat," she said.

"Thee knowest damn well thou hast sat upon my hat. What is thee going to do about it?"

"I am going to return it to thee," she replied, with such a beatific smile as only angels wear. Ned, for once speechless with anger, got up and left the car. Memories such as these always come into my head whenever I think of Ned Campion. But to get on with my story.

Campion said to me, "Eddie, we have been friends for almost fifty years and I don't think I have ever asked you to do me a favor." "I don't think you have," I replied. "Well, I'm going to now, and I want you to do it." Feeling quite certain that in five minutes I should be making out a check for five hundred dollars, I waited. He waited. "I'll tell you what I want," he said. "I want you to write a short introduction to a volume of *The Letters of Madame de Sévigné* which J. P. Horn & Company" (with whom he was then associated) "are going to publish. We want your name on the title-page," he continued.

I was in just five hundred dollars, or, looked at another way, I was being paid just that sum for two evenings' pleasant work. I knew very little about Madame de Sévigné. I had read some of her most famous letters, in French, forty, say fifty years before, and during the previous summer I had spent some weeks in Paris and had passed several pleasant mornings in the Musée Carnavalet, from which famous *hôtel* many of her letters were sent. I could without difficulty and with profit to myself

53

renew my slender acquaintance with the subject. So after a few moments' demurral I agreed to take on the job.

But the end was not yet. Campion continued: "I knew you would; I told Horn so. But this must be a matter of business. How much are you going to charge us?"

You could have knocked me down with a feather. "Why, Ned, nothing," I replied. "I never accept a fee for odd jobs like this; that's why I get so many of 'em."

"Oh, but that won't do," he continued; "we expect to pay you, of course."

I saw he was quite in earnest, and I said, "I 'll tell you what: when the book is published send me ten copies." (I supposed that the letters would be published in one volume.) "I 'll give them away as presents to my friends."

"Well, Eddie, that's noble of you, and very generous."

So the matter was left that way, and after a few minutes' further conversation, in which we told each other what fine fellows we were, I left the store — in five hundred dollars, and, as I thought, with ten nice books to give away at Christmas.

I did the little job, had a pleasant time doing it, sent in my manuscript, read the proofs some months later, smiling as I did so.

It was, I think, almost a year later that one day a big black man entered my office carrying a heavy bundle about the size of a steamer trunk. "Your name Newton?" he inquired. I admitted it was. "Books," he said, dropping the package on the floor with a thud. "Not for me, I think." "I don't know nothing about that; Newton's the name." — and he departed. I had the package opened, and there were revealed ten *sets* of the Carnavalet Edition of *The Letters of Madame de Sévigné*, seven volumes to a set, handsomely printed and well bound, "limited to fifteen hundred numbered sets" and selling at retail for fifty dollars a set!

After this recital, it only remains for me to say that this particular edition is one without which no gentleman's library is complete.

These memories, and many more, flashed through my mind as I stood with bowed head at the bier of my friend. May angels guard him. I have never been able, quite, to make up my mind as to the sex of angels, but if they are virgins — as they appear to be in pictures — let them watch their step or Ned 'll make matrons of 'em.

V

NELSON

WHEN Molière made one of his characters exclaim, "*Nous avons changé tout cela!*" he certainly — in the words of a Lady Mayoress of New York — said a mouthful. And if change was a characteristic of Molière's day, how much more so is it of ours! Thanks to democracy and the war, and to the horrors of peace, of votes for women, and of prohibition, and to the utter collapse of fundamentalism with all that it connotes, the world has begun to spin so furiously that it makes one dizzy to think of it. Wise men don't; realizing that it is quite hopeless to attempt to catch up with it, they deliberately turn their backs upon the present and live behind the times.

To escape from the speed and noise and vulgarity of to-day into the calm of the eighteenth century is a great delight. It was the last age in which people really lived. I know that W. S. Gilbert speaks disparagingly of

> The idiot who praises, with enthusiastic tone,
> All centuries but this and every country but his own,

but nevertheless that is what I am going to do. I am going to forget the telephone and the radio and all the other time-and-distance-annihilating devices, and think of a day and a country where people dined and wined and talked, of a time when conversation was not a lost art. I ask you to think, with me, of *James Woodforde's Diary*, recently published and read, in five stout and interesting volumes about nothing whatever but the life of a country parson *and what he ate*. Why are biographies and memoirs, especially of the eighteenth century, so popular? Is it not because they treat of times which are remote enough and different enough from our own to be interesting and yet sufficiently near us to be understandable? And for the same reason the nineteenth century is now coming into its own: witness the renaissance of Trollope. His best work was done in the eighteen-sixties and eighteen-seventies, yet his England is almost as remote as the England of Henry Fielding. I have said elsewhere, and I wish to repeat, that no English novelist has so many first-class novels to his credit as has Anthony Trollope.

Agnes Repplier, our most distinguished "bluestocking," published some years ago a delightful little volume of essays which she called *A Happy Half Century*. It is a book full of charm and humor; only its author could have written it. Miss Repplier's chosen half century is the last twenty-five years of the eighteenth and the first twenty-five years of the nineteenth century. I, too, love to lose myself in that period; and Amy Lowell, that rare spirit, had great affection for it. How remote it is! How far away it seems! It was the age of *personal* romance. We also live in an age of romance, but it is *mechanical* romance. Every wonder of to-day is connected with a tube or with a coil of wire which may be, and probably is, a magnet; but the magnet of other days — a woman, that is — no longer draws us as she once did; she merely shocks us. We feel that we have touched a live wire; and very likely we have. Time was when an uplifted skirt revealing a pretty silken ankle — to the knee, almost — gave one a pleasant thrill; now we regard a woman's leg to the waist as so much cold meat. Young girls of the present day have seemingly forgotten, or have never heard that, as George Meredith says, "Mystery is woman's redoubtable weapon." They now leave nothing to our imagination. Will it be remembered that Sir Austin Feverel thought it necessary to instruct his son that a woman's legs are, in all essentials, very like our own? He said that the ballet was imported from France for the instruction of inquiring youth.

I am thinking of the age of the stagecoach, of the time when, if one was in a great hurry, one hired a post chaise — now, one "goes by air." Reform — that curse, the last refuge of a scoundrel — had not yet set in; a man could raise a thirst and satisfy it. Every man had his price and did not hesitate to state it. What was the price of a first-class banker two years ago? They came so high that only the very rich could afford to own one. The rest of us had to club together to get one. (I don't much like the word "club," it is too reminiscent.)

NELSON

In these days of vaunted efficiency we can do pretty much everything except live. Men who can and should escape from the cares of business do not do so because they would find themselves without recourse. They do not understand that living is, in itself, an art. It is their fixed determination to relax to-morrow — which never comes.

> I 'll live to-morrow
> You delaying cry —
> In what far country
> Does to-morrow lie?

For me, at all events, it lies "in England's green and pleasant land"; in the England of Jane Austen — before Trafalgar and Waterloo, certainly before the Reform Bill. Only upon the comic-opera stage are our political problems solved with any certainty.

> When Wellington thrashed Bonaparte,
> As every child can tell,
> The House of Peers, throughout the war,
> Did nothing in particular,
> And did it very well.
> Yet Britain set the world ablaze
> In good King George's glorious days!

When, later, the House of Commons took matters in hand, we had the Crimea — well named, Crime-a.

And now, by indirection, I arrive at my subject — Nelson; being led thereto not, I think, by reading Barrington's *Divine Lady*, so much as by a re-reading of Amy Lowell's *Can Grande's Castle*, with particular emphasis upon two chapters — or cantos, if the book be poetry, which it is: "Hedge Island," which is the England of Mr. Pickwick and Sam Weller, and "Sea Blue and Blood Red," which is Nelson. England! my spiritual home, where the hedge-bordered highways always led to a "George" or a "Lion" or a "Bull" or a "Crown," or some other inn with its generous hospitality.

> Whoe'er has travell'd life's dull round,
> Where'er his stages may have been,
> May sigh to think he still has found
> The warmest welcome at an inn.

Four lines merely, but it makes Shenstone immortal; two lines only, of real poetry, will frequently do it.

I am thinking of England of the past. And it was to safeguard this lovely land that Nelson

fought and bled and died, and now stands a-top
of a tall shaft, a very tall shaft, in Trafalgar
Square. How many great triumphs England's
navy has to its credit any Englishman will tell
you, but the world at large thinks chiefly of two:
that of Drake over the Spanish Armada, and
Nelson over the combined fleets of France and
Spain created by Napoleon for the destruction
of all that Englishmen hold dear.

Trafalgar is a small cape on the southern
coast of Spain, projecting into the Atlantic between Cadiz and the Strait of Gibraltar. Off
this cape on October 21, 1805, the great battle
was fought, and, if the total overthrow of Napoleon's hopes was deferred until the Battle of
Waterloo ten years later, Nelson had done his
part. There is nothing finer, nothing more
characteristically English than the death of
Nelson, in song and in fact. He planned the
battle and then retired to his cabin and wrote the
following prayer: —

May the great God, whom I worship, grant to my
country, and for the benefit of Europe in general, a
great and glorious victory, and may no misconduct
in any one tarnish it; and may humanity after vic-

tory be the predominant feature in the British Fleet! For myself individually, I commit my life to Him that made me; and may his blessing alight on my endeavors for serving my country faithfully! To Him I resign myself, and the just cause which is entrusted to me to defend. Amen, Amen, Amen.

This is fundamentalism at its glorious best. *Nous avons changé tout cela* also. It could not be helped, it had to come, but the world has lost something inexpressibly precious. What shall we put in its place? "If there were no God we should have to invent one," said a very wise man.

It is commonplace to say that all England is emotional with history, but this is especially true of the country round about Portsmouth. One pleasant Sunday, not long ago, we, my wife and I, were motoring through the "New Forest," — "new" forest, forsooth; it was already old in the time of the Conqueror, — when it occurred to us to go on to Portsmouth and visit Nelson's old flagship, the *Victory*. On our way we spent several pleasant hours in the little-known but fascinating hamlet, Bucklers Hard, where many of Nelson's ships were built and launched upon a stream which is now so silted up that at low water it will scarcely float a rowboat. The *Victory*, certainly the most famous of the "wooden walls of England," after Trafalgar never again engaged an enemy but was used as a training ship; ultimately, with the passage of a century or more, becoming a rats' sanctuary. Then someone had the bright idea of floating the ship to a famous dry dock, built in the time of Charles the Second, in the great naval harbor of Portsmouth, and there reconditioning her into a shrine. I happened to be in England at the time when this good work was begun and was happy to make a small contribution to that end.

We boarded the magnificent old battleship with reverence and climbed over her from stem to stern — quite a chore, and a most interesting one. Her interior fittings have all been faithfully and tastefully restored — what if her long rows of cannon are now of wood, painted black? They were not of wood on that fateful day when Nelson won his greatest and final victory. "England expects that every man will do his duty" was the signal that he flew. And every man did. Knowing full well that the enemy had sharpshooters in the shrouds of the *Redoubtable*, with which his ship was engaged, Nelson, disdaining the disguise of a common seaman, insisted upon remaining on deck, in full uniform, for the encouragement of his crew. Then, if ever, death loved a shining mark. A rifle-ball shattered his spine. "They have done for me at last, Hardy," he exclaimed. "My backbone is shot through." He was taken below into the cockpit and expired in awful agony, with the words, "Thank God I have done my duty; kiss me, Hardy," on his lips. A group of realistic Madame Tussaud waxwork, dimly lit with what appear to be old-fashioned lanthorns, marks the place where he died. No single thing that I have ever seen has so moved me. It is something, or nothing, to see such a spot — as one happens to be constituted.

In the log of the *Victory* is this brief, but sufficient, entry: "Partial firing continued until 4.30, when a victory having been reported to the Right Honorable Lord Viscount Nelson, K.B., he died of his wound."

Only a man of small stature such as Nelson was could stand upright between decks, even in such an important vessel as the *Victory*. Captain Hardy, whose name will always be associated with Nelson's, was a very tall man: in order that he might stand upright, a small hole was cut in the main deck through which he could stick his head. This, in effect, enabled him to be in two places at once, no small advantage when so many orders were given by word of mouth.

No hero, in a land of heroes, makes half the appeal that Nelson does; perhaps because he was a great lover as well as a great fighter. "I leave Lady Hamilton and my daughter Horatia as a legacy to my country." He lost an eye in one battle and an arm in another. So much the better. When told, on one occasion, that his commanding officer had signaled "Retire," he raised his glass to his blind eye and said, "I see no such signal; let the fighting continue." He could not yield his sword, he said, he had lost his sword arm; he, in fact, never had occasion to do so: his life was a series of triumphs, culminating at Trafalgar. After the battle, the French Admiral, Villeneuve, afraid to meet the rage of his master, committed suicide. It was the beginning of the end of Napoleon.

I have at hand no means of knowing how large the *Victory* is. To say that she is a big vessel is to say nothing. Nor do I know how many men constituted her crew. When the *Royal George*, in 1782, keeled over and foundered in Portsmouth Harbor, she had, according to Cowper's famous poem, eight hundred souls on board. The fighting strength of the *Victory* may have been as many. They must have been packed in like the traditional sardine. Much space was required for ammunition and supplies of all kinds, for food, and for water. There was no ventilation; conditions must have been intolerable. Dr. Johnson once said that no man would go to sea who had the contrivance to get himself thrown into a jail, for life at sea was very like life in a jail, with the added chance of being drowned — and, he might have added, — of a fighting ship, — of being killed. The Admiral's quarters, on the other hand, were rather fine; he had a small deck or "walk" to himself over the stern, a comfortable cabin, and an excellent dining room or drawing-room:

one fancies that it was much used. Moreover, the profits resulting from a successful battle were enormous. This is a world in which it hardly pays to be the under dog.

A week later, on a Sunday afternoon, we went to a service in the Wren Chapel at Greenwich, "the green town," on the Thames.

> On Thames's bank, in silent thought we stood,
> Where Greenwich smiles upon the silver flood;
> In pleasing dreams the glorious age renew,
> And call Britannia's victories to view.

Henry the Eighth was born here. Anne Boleyn lived here, happily, for a few months; here Elizabeth was born and had her home for a time. James the First lived here; so did Charles the First. It was too far from the ladies and the theatres to please Charles the Second, and fell into decay. Then Wren's services were requisitioned and a new Greenwich arose. Queen Anne's home it then became, and it is now the Navy's and Nelson's. A picture gallery and a museum are devoted to him. Modern history, as well as longitude, begins at Greenwich. Why is it a *terra incognita* to most Londoners? They go to the Abbey occasionally, for the Abbey is less a church than an epitome of English history. They go to the Tower, rather reluctantly, — and I don't blame them much, — with friends from overseas; but Greenwich, which is one of the most magnificent things in London, they leave severely alone. Reader, when you have an opportunity, visit Greenwich, but first get the vista from the little green park on the other side of the River. Then go to the "Painted Hall" and, in reflective mood, look at the Nelson relics; the Wren Chapel alone is worth the journey.

VI

THE VOICE OF THE HADMIRAL

With apologies to the Shade of Thomas Hardy and making obeisance to the "Dictionary of National Biography."

The reader is to suppose that he is overhearing the conversation of two old salts who are lounging upon the waterside at Portsmouth, one day in January, 1806. The "Victory," bearing every evidence of battle, has been made fast to the quay not far off.

Hit 's a fine daie, Bill. 'Ave you 'eard the news?

Hi 've seen worse. Wot news? Trafalgar 's no news, no more.

Trafalgar's news 'll keep fresh for some time, my matey — longer nor the body of the Hadmiral.

Hit 's to be put hin Paul's, Hi 'ear, hin a marble coffing, hafter a showin' of the body and a staite funeral.

Hi 'eard has much. 'Ow long hafter a man's

death his 'is body decent to show to the naked eye — makin' no mention of 'is nose?

Hit hall depends hon 'ow hit 's kep'. The Hadmiral's could 'ave kep' forhever — savin' for one little circumstance wot halters caises.

Meanin', no doubt, the 'ot weather and the distance 'ome from the scene of haction.

Meanin' th' hunkonkerable luv hof grog wot his the hinhalienable right hof hevery British tar hafloat hor hon shore.

Wot 's that to do with Hadmiral wot 's flew 'is last signal?

Much, hif Hi 'm correctly tole — han Hi got the story from one of the men wot 's to pull the rope of the gun kerrige with the coffing in the funeral procession. Hafter the haction they sinks corpses by scores while chapling reads from the Good Book, and they makes neat the 'ole ship — wots name 's never to be forgot while mem'ry 'olds. But Hadmiral 'es set hupright hin a cask with 'is 'ed between 'is knees and spirits poured hover 'im to keep 'im sweet.

Spirits poured hover 'im!

Yus! Then 'es coopered hup has safe has a church — but fur the hunkonkerable thirst wot

will break out hin a man hon sea hor hon
shore.

Wot's that to do with Hadmiral wot's flew
'is last signal?

Much. *They broached the cask with a gimlet.*
'T is crime, they say, to let so much good licker go
to waiste. Han Hi'm tole the voice hof the
Hadmiral was 'eard from hinside the cask:
"*Drink 'earty, my lads, drink 'earty,*" hit says:
"*Hi never begrudge men wot's done their duty a
drop o' grog. Wot hif hi shrivel!*"

Which his like Hadmiral — always thinkin'
hof 'is men fust and self haafter.

VII

ANTHONY TROLLOPE

ALL good Trollopeans will welcome this book.[1]
It is curious that only three books should have
been written about Anthony Trollope, and it is
hardly less curious that I should have read two
of them in manuscript. In 1912, when I was in
London, John Lane, the publisher, knowing my
interest in Trollope, asked me if I would read a
book about him, by T. H. S. Escott, and give
him my opinion of it. I consented, and waded
through a pile of manuscript that filled a good-
sized suitcase. My report was not unfavorable:
I said that the book would probably pay its way;
Lane accepted it, and my opinion was justified.

Several years ago, I was sitting with my friend
Michael Sadleir; he remarked that Escott's book
was the only book on Trollope and it was high
time there was another. "Why don't you write

[1] *Anthony Trollope: A Commentary*, by Michael Sadleir,
Houghton Mifflin Co.

it?" I inquired. "You have the material, the knowledge, and the enthusiasm; you do it." Naturally, when Mr. Sadleir asked me to read his book and write an introduction to it, I felt bound to do so; and as I read, the duty became a pleasure.

The world is divided into Trollopeans — and others. If you, reader, are not one of us, hasten to become one, for there are few pleasures equal to that of knowing Trollope through and through, as Sadleir does, and as Tinker (of Yale) does, and as Osgood (of Princeton) does, and — I should like to add — as I do. I do not say that Trollope is our greatest novelist; I know that he is not, but I can read him with delight when I can't read anyone else.

Anthony Trollope died on December 6, 1882. Already a little outmoded before his death, the publication of his *Autobiography* just simply mutilated his reputation, seemingly forever. People stopped reading him; finally, the generation that had known and read and enjoyed his books as they were published passed away, and was followed by another that knew nothing and desired to know nothing of him; so that, in the

late nineties in London, if one recommended
Trollope, he was met by a stare and "Oh, that
old Victorian who used to write at so much an
hour, or so many words a minute, or whatever it
was! No, I care nothing about him." But he
continued to have his admirers in America, and
to-day we are a noble band — as far as numbers are concerned. And we have quality, too.
Anyone getting into an argument about Trollope
with Henry S. Drinker, Jr., is likely to remember
the encounter. I doubt if Michael Sadleir,
Trollope's official bibliographer, knows very
much more of his subject than Carroll A. Wilson,
of New York. Morris L. Parrish has a complete
set of Trollope in "Parrish condition" — every
bookseller knows what that means. Barton
Currie has another. Spencer Van B. Nichols is
a real enthusiast — acquire a copy of his delightful little volume, *The Significance of Anthony
Trollope*. William J. Serrill claims to have read
all or almost all of Trollope aloud. I am men-
tioning only personal friends.

But I doubt if Trollope would have called us a
"noble band." During his lifetime, there being
no international copyright, or next to none, we

CARICATURE OF A GREAT NOVELIST, ANTHONY
TROLLOPE
By "Spy" (Leslie Ward)

stole his books right and left, and paid him not a single penny. But remember, Shade of Anthony, that when your own beloved English went back on you and called you superficial, and trivial and monotonous and commonplace and vulgar, without charm or imagination, we never did: we kept your torch alight, and now the English are returning to an author we Americans never deserted.

Trollope's mother (bless her stout heart!) kept her family from starving by making fun of us in her first book, *Domestic Manners of the Americans* (1832). I "guess" we were pretty raw in those days. And if there is a good deal about Mrs. Trollope and her novels in this book, it will be remembered, as Mr. Sadleir says, "that from her books came, in reality, the greater books of her son, and while his live those that prepared their way should not be altogether forgotten."

And so it is that after almost fifty years of neglect Trollope is again coming into his own, and is being read when those whom we once called great Victorians are neglected. Mr. Sadleir calls the opening chapter of his book, "The Voice of an Epoch": it reads like a particularly brilliant chapter out of Justin McCarthy's *History of Our Own Times*. Turning these considered pages, we see that we are to-day in manners, and in morals too, further away from the decorous times of Queen Victoria — a time when an archbishop could preach a sermon against sensational novelists and attack novel-reading as a practice pernicious in the young — than we are from the period of the Regency. This is very curious.

Whether a man writes well or ill, he always writes for his own time, and as a rule his work dies with him; when it survives him a century or more, we say that the man had genius. Trollope was a genius, but seemingly of so commonplace a type (if the phrase be permitted) that he never suspected it — nor did his contemporaries. For the greater part of his life he was a "civil servant" in the General Post Office, just as our own Herman Melville came to be a clerk in the New York Custom House; we now know that the author of *Moby Dick* was a genius too.

It is the aim of Sadleir's book to tell not only how and why Trollope has survived his own generation and the one next following, but to shed some side lights upon his life, lights which

from their very nature one could hardly expect
to get from the fascinating and autodestroying
Autobiography.

People interested Trollope, interested him
enormously; cities did not, particularly; nor did
the country, except as a place in or on which to
hunt the fox. But individuals interested him,
and not individuals only, but families, and
several generations of families. Not only is
Trollope a portrait painter, but he is a biographer
also. Trollope's novels are, the best of them,
biographies; and as such they are unique. And
he has described, faultlessly, the social life of a
period now, alas! no more; he is also a humorist
— and humor is an invaluable quality in a novelist. All through his books are scenes which keep
one in a contented smile (we Trollopeans are too
sophisticated to laugh aloud). I think no more
amusing chapters were ever written than the
two describing Mrs. Proudie's reception in *Barchester Towers*. And Trollope is quite ready to
turn the shafts of his humor against himself.
Speaking of the great exhibition of 1851, he says:
"I mean to exhibit four three-volume novels —
all failures."

Trollope was also a realist; not a realist in the Continental-European sense, — a nastyist, — but in the sense that he secures his effects by the simplest and most direct means. It was the great Sir Walter who, in his criticism of Jane Austen, said that "he could do the big bowwow stuff as well as any fellow going, but in the portrayal of daily life he was deficient." It is in this delineation of daily life that Trollope excels, and he had a delicacy which was seemingly at variance with his own bluff and rather combative nature. He could paint a finished portrait, or make a sketch so lifelike that we cannot forget it.

Of no important character in fiction is so little actually said as of the Duke of Omnium, yet few Dukes in history do we know better than him. The Duke had his failings, no doubt, but he was nevertheless a Duke and entitled to the utmost respect; even Lady Lufton curtseyed "low" to him. The encounter between him and Lady Lufton, at the top of Miss Dunstable's staircase, is one of the best things Trollope ever did. He was a great Duke, but it will be remembered that Lady Lufton, who was by comparison a nobody, "was held by all the world to have had the best of the encounter." Consider, too, the delicacy of the opening chapters of *Barchester Towers* where the worldly Archdeacon drops upon his knees at the bedside of his dying father, praying that his life may be prolonged, yet knowing that, if it be prolonged, he, the Archdeacon, will lose the chance of a lifetime: no bishopric will be his.

Trollope loves to portray crimes not within the reach of any law. With these he invariably deals, as an Englishman should, with his fists — as when Crosbie, in *The Small House at Allington*, having jilted Lily Dale, gets a thrashing at the hands of Johnny Eames on the railway platform at Paddington. And I have always derived much satisfaction from that scene in Scumberg's Hotel in *Is He Popenjoy?* where the Dean takes the Marquis, the father of Popenjoy, and, after thoroughly shaking him, throws him into an empty fireplace. Personally, I should have preferred a bed of hot coals in that fireplace, but Trollope, no doubt, knew best.

One of the best things in Sadleir's book is his appreciation of *Doctor Thorne*, which will delight the Trollopean. I may truly say that this novel is the only novel upon reading which tears invariably come into my eyes: tears of joy that Mary Thorne should, at last, not only get her lover, but bring to him a sum of money that restores his family to its proper position in the county — a sum which even the De Courcy interest admits to be magnificent. If Frank Gresham and Mary Thorne do not "live happily ever after," it certainly is not Trollope's fault.

I was amazed to discover that Sir Arthur Quiller-Couch calls Johnny Eames "a little bounder." He would, of course, be a little bounder to the great Duke of Omnium, but that "Q," a mere college professor, should so call him is a pity. We shall next hear of someone calling Joe Gargery a cad.

I cannot close without reference to a little paper that appeared some years ago in the *Atlantic Monthly*, entitled "Barsetshire and the War," by Miss Helen Bowen, a lady I should have known but did not. In this paper some of the chief characters in the novels were made to carry on as they certainly would have done had the war come in their time. The Reverend

Mark Robarts went out with a cavalry regiment and grumbled at life in the trenches, but did his duty manfully. . . . Lily Dale and Mary Thorne and Lucy Robarts became nurses, of course: no more fascinating and curing and compensating could possibly have crossed the Channel. . . . The Reverend Mr. Crawley (bless his heart!) recruited a whole company of brickmakers from Hogglestock and tramped with them the miry roads of Flanders, chanting Euripides. . . . Mr. Slope was at first a pacifist, but, quickly sensing the unpopularity of that course, shifted to preaching patriotic sermons in the vicinity of the New Road. It was not necessary for him to go to the front: he could do his duty without quitting his comfortable house in Baker Street. . . . All those fearless, straight-riding country gentlemen went promptly to the front, and most of them did not come back. . . . Archdeacon Grantley, having been refused active service on account of his age, threw himself into the work of increasing the food production, as did Lord De Guest, and Squire Dale, and a host of others. . . . The Duke's children, the sons of "Planty Pall" and Lady Glencora, greatly distinguished themselves: they would, of course. And as the Countess De Courcy and Lady Alexandrina were in Baden-Baden when the war broke out, they were interned throughout its length. Good! . . . Lily Dale found Johnny Eames badly wounded in a hospital, and at last, discovering there was something godlike about him, scratched "O. M." out of her book. What a relief! And especially note the delicacy of this touch. Griselda Grantley made her sacrifices also. Throughout the whole period of the war, she had only two women to maid her.

What would I not give to have written this exquisite summary! But, not being able to write it, I have, at least, the pleasure of quoting it.

Mr. Sadleir is a student, an author, a publisher, and a collector. His specialty as a collector is the three-volume novel of the time of Victoria — the "three-decker," as it is called; it is an intricate and fascinating subject. The initiated will know his excellent book, *Excursions in Victorian Bibliography*. From the point of view of the book-collector, Trollope is difficult beyond words. His early novels are practically unobtainable in any condition, and when they are discovered they are usually "bound," and not too well. Most of his books promptly went into the "libraries," where they were read to rags. Still, in one way or another, they can be had. I have every book Trollope ever wrote, and I rejoice in my possession — no books give me greater pleasure.

VIII

"ROBINSON CRUSOE"

WHEN a book [1] by an American scholar is favorably reviewed in the *London Times Literary Supplement* one may conclude that the work has merit; so much merit, in fact, that the reviewer has been unable to "dust the varlet's jacket" as he, no doubt, intended to do at the outset. My reader will perhaps remember that when Macaulay heard that John Wilson Croker was busying himself with a new edition of Boswell's *Life of Johnson*, he wrote his sister that he would review the book and dust the editor's (whom he called a varlet) jacket thoroughly. He did so, and much critical work in England is still done in this spirit; especially if the author under review happens to be an American, or even, more unluckily, if he is not an alumnus of either of the two great universities.

[1] *Robinson Crusoe and Its Printing*, by Henry Clinton Hutchins, Columbia University Press.

"ROBINSON CRUSOE"

"More poets yet," I heard him say,
Arming his heavy hand to slay.

I am not greatly concerned with what a reviewer can do to a poet. If the poet deserves to survive, no critic can slay him. But Henry Clinton Hutchins is a scholar and a bibliographer and these are to a *Times* reviewer what a red rag is generally thought to be to a bull. My friend has escaped very handsomely and I congratulate him. In *Robinson Crusoe and Its Printing* we have a scholarly presentation of many difficult literary and bibliographical problems, including a dissertation upon the proper use of the perplexing terms "edition" and "issue," to which I, having practically no bibliographical sense whatever, shall merely allude and pass on.

I was honored by being asked to write an Introduction, which I did with ease (no recommendation) and pleasure, and even I almost escaped the "Bull" (meaning the *Times* reviewer), for my Introduction is described — and not ironically I hope — as "entertaining." And this is what I said: —

One swallow does not make a summer — certainly not; yet it will be clear to the most casual observer that the appearance of a swallow proves that it is no longer midwinter. And the appearance of this Bibliography of one of the world's great romances — if that be the best word to describe Defoe's masterpiece — suggests that there must be something wrong in the diagnosis that we Americans are a sordid, money-grubbing race wholly given over to "efficiency." In a word, that we are wholly materialistic. I deny it; the reverse is the fact. The diagnosis is European in its origin, and we have rested quietly under the imputation all too long; sometimes we have even seemed to agree with it. This shows the value of iteration : if we are told a thing, no matter how preposterous it may be, often enough, we come to believe it. The appearance of this Bibliography, which is entirely a labor of love, is evidence to the contrary.

Dr. Johnson called a lexicographer "a harmless drudge." He ought to have known, for he was one; and if he had so far forgotten himself as to call my friend Mr. Hutchins by the same name, he would, I think, turning the leaves of this volume, have added more kindly, "Here is scholarship working without hope of reward."

It is not for me to point out the unique merits of *Robinson Crusoe*, "either with or without the O." Its place in English literature, in all literature, is secure. It is not my favorite book: I do not often turn to it when I am anxious to forget my own problems in those of another, as did the old manservant in *The Moonstone;* but I am sure others have done so, for nothing happens in fiction that does not happen in real life.

"The greatest boy's book ever written," it has been called; it may be so, but it is much more than this, or if it be a boy's book, it is so in the sense that *The Arabian Nights* is a child's book, which everyone knows it is not: children, when *The Arabian Nights* was written, were of little more value than flies. The idea that *Robinson Crusoe* was "a boy's book" would have filled Defoe with amazement. Of what use for him to develop his theories of the mechanic arts, the uses of solitude and of society, the pleasure of refreshing sleep after fatigue, and much moralizing, if the book were only intended for boys? "I read it when a boy," you will hear someone say in reply to your question whether he has read this or that great book: is it possible that our reading as boys was better than our reading as men? I sometimes fear that it is so.

Mr. Hutchins has described my copy of the first edition (which was once Congreve's) and also my copy of *Heathcot's Intelligence*,[1] the newspaper in which *Crusoe* ran serially during the first year of its publication; and as, with all his skill and investigation, he does not seem to have discovered another copy except the severely damaged example in the British Museum, I suppose I may refer to mine as almost unique; but I note with interest that he does *not* refer to another copy I own, namely an edition published in New York by G. W. Carleton and Co. in 1872, in which in that same year I first read the immortal story.

No reference to *Robinson Crusoe* would be complete unless mention was made of the frontispiece of the first edition: the famous copperplate illustration by Clark and Pine, represent-

[1] Now don't some snippy reviewer of these papers rise up and say this should be Heathcote's, not Heathcot's. The fact is the early numbers are spelled one way, the later, another.

JIMMY HATLO VISUALIZES THE AUTHOR OF "THE
AMENITIES OF BOOK-COLLECTING"

ing the poor castaway in what must have been a remarkably trying costume for hot weather — which we are assured the weather was at the time of the shipwreck. It shows him dressed in a jacket and trousers of sheepskin, with no shoes or stockings on, a gun over each shoulder, and a sword most inconveniently worn. This illustration has outlasted several centuries of criticism. We always look for it and are disappointed when we do not find it: when Crusoe appears on the stage we are reminded of it, whether the impersonator be a man or, as is usual, a woman. It has come to be the accepted portrait; no legend is required: one knows that he is looking at Robinson Crusoe.

But more wonderful than the costume itself are its surprising attributes; for we read on page fifty-five: "I pulled off my clothes, for the weather was hot to extremity," and, plunging into the water, swam out to the ship, which in the picture seems so far to have withstood the buffetings of an angry sea. Immediately on reaching the ship, which he does on the next page, he goes "to the bread room" and, forgetful that he had no clothes on, "fills his pockets with bisket," which he munches while he goes about his business. In several modern editions this amusing blunder is corrected and the passage suggests that Crusoe swam to the boat in his linen breeches and stockings.

Reproduced in one way or another in most of the reprints of the book, this famous picture has no place in the Carleton edition, a badly dog-eared and "shaken" volume, and I have always resented its omission. As I turn the pages of my childhood's copy, half a century drops from my shoulders; and in imagination I see myself a rather delicate, pale, slender little lad in Fort Scott, Kansas, poring over the book and wondering — for a child's world is full of wonder.

And looking at the pictures. All books are the better for pictures; they assist one's imagination wonderfully. In my *Crusoe* the hero has been dashed by a great wave against a mast; behind it a seaman is praying. There is another of the semicircular stockade, with the entrance not by a door but by a short ladder which could be pulled up. There is another of R. C. carrying a turtle about the size of a Saratoga trunk; and there is — my God! there is the print of a man's naked foot upon the sand, the most realistic scene in all fiction. But enough. I don't think I ever finished the book, — it grows a bit tiresome towards the end, — but I remember being much affected by Friday's discovery of his old father, and being melted to tears when the poor, dear, faithful servant and companion was killed. He served as a target, you will remember, for three hundred arrows, three of which reached their mark.

How amazed Defoe would be if he could take up this Bibliography and follow the fortunes, not of Crusoe and his man Friday, but of a mere word through several pages: the word "apyly" or "pilate," or "pilot," for instance; and finally when a matter of life and death seems to hang upon a colon, — not that unpleasant thing we carry about in our insides, but a mark of punctuation; a "stop," our English friends call it, — or even half a colon.

This Bibliography is not intended for the average reader, be he gentle or simple. It is intended as a tool for the scholar, a weapon for the bookseller, a suit of armor for the collector; and of its kind I doubt if they have ever seen a better. There are interesting disquisitions on publishers and printers, on the vexed point of "editions" and "issues," on papers, and on types. In a word, it is just what this kind of a book should be: exact, painstaking, and scholarly. Or, to put the matter another way, it is such a book as I could not have written had my life depended upon it. But it is something to be able to appreciate it, and it is much to be asked to write an Introduction to it.

IX

BURTON'S "ANATOMY" AND ANOTHER

I HAVE a confession to make. Many years ago, in a merry mood, I wrote a silly paragraph which I now wish to withdraw. Speaking of Burton's *Anatomy of Melancholy*, — misnamed if a book ever was, — I quoted Dr. Johnson's remark that "it was the only book that ever took him out of bed two hours earlier than he wished to rise." I should never have dared to oppose the Doctor in the flesh, but as he is and has been lying in the Abbey, very comfortably I hope, for a century and a half, I flippantly retorted that "that same book put me very promptly to sleep"; that "I kept it by my bedside for that purpose." Now, the fact is that at the time I don't think I had ever read ten consecutive pages of this seventeenth-century classic. When a great man criticizes a book favorably, or unfavorably, it is always well for one to stop, look, and listen. This I did not do.

At the time I made this silly remark, the book was not, however, entirely unknown to me. I had a good copy of the first edition, and that particular edition is not easy to read. It is an ugly, dumpy quarto volume, printed at Oxford in 1621; the type is small, and its every page bristles with Latin quotations in italics; moreover, the glosses on the outer and lower margins of the page, in still smaller type, also in Latin, are trying to the last degree. Its full title, too, is rather appalling: *The Anatomy of Melancholy, What It Is, With All Kinds, Causes, Symptoms, Prognostica, And Several Cures Of It, In Three Main Partitions.* . . . There is a lot more, but this will serve. What ignorant man but would shy at such a book? And that is exactly what I did.

It was not until some years after I had made my jejune criticism that, one evening at the dinner table of Paul Jordan-Smith, in Hollywood, California, my distinguished host took me severely to task for my remark and said, "I don't believe you ever read the book." I confessed that I had not, and I excused myself as best I could by saying that I hated an author who concealed his best stories in a learned language, *à la* Gibbon, as I suspected old Burton of doing. "Very well," said Jordan-Smith; "some of these days I shall send you a well-printed copy of the book in which all these Latin tags, which so offend you, are translated." Our conversation was interrupted at this point and we passed on to other subjects.

A year later, Holbrook Jackson, an English scholar well known to me from his book, *The Eighteen Nineties*, — which after twenty years remains the best book of literary criticism of the period, — brought out his amazing book, *The Anatomy of Bibliomania*. It is, not in its subject but in its style, quite as remarkable as is the more famous *Anatomy*, and I make no doubt will be very much alive when the scribblings of all other writers on the pleasure of collecting and reading books are forgotten. Holbrook Jackson's work is in two portly volumes, and its style is purposely archaic; for this reason it is not, at first, too easy to read; then one remembers that he is following his seventeenth-century exemplar. Immediately upon securing and reading Mr. Jackson's book, I wrote him a letter telling him of my great delight in it, and demanding to know, honestly, was he one man or many? for I thought he might be a "whole synod" of readers. Subsequently I made Jackson's acquaintance in London, and he told me that his *Anatomy* was the result of twenty years' close reading. I should have believed him had he said a hundred. His book was very inadequately reviewed in the *Times Literary Supplement*, for the reason that its editor is steeped in "port and prejudice" against any author who has not the hall mark of Oxford or Cambridge. "Beware of the man of one book." Holbrook Jackson's one book — out of thousands — is Burton's *Anatomy of Melancholy*. He has edited and published an edition in the Everyman Series in three volumes. (I boast a presentation copy.)

On my return from London, I found a parcel from Paul Jordan-Smith; opening it, I found his edition of old Burton in one stout volume, published in New York, by Farrar and Rinehart. In this edition my friend was assisted by, or gave his assistance to, Floyd Dell. Anyhow, between them they have produced a Burton's

Anatomy which I have read with delight, not from cover to cover, — for, as Dr. Johnson once inquired, "Who reads a book through?" — but I have read most of it once and parts of it several times. But the book does not require my indorsement. Further: on the table before me is another book, *Bibliographia Burtoniana*, a study of old Burton's *Anatomy*, by Paul Jordan-Smith (the Stanford University Press). The book is a delightful essay, a biography and a bibliography; no good Burtonian will be without it.

Now, reader, "believe it or not," at this point in my writing I was interrupted by my mentor, who, sitting on the other side of the evening lamp, lifted herself out of her book to inquire what was I doing?

"A few last pages, on Burton's *Anatomy*, for my *End Papers*," I replied.

"I have just this moment read Byron's comment upon that book. What a coincidence! Here it is."

Whereupon she handed me the volume she was reading — Volume I of *The Life, Letters and Poems of Lord Byron*, London, 1832; and there, on page 144, I read: —

Burton's *Anatomy* is, in my opinion, most useful to a man who wishes to acquire the reputation of being well read with the least trouble. *It is the most amusing and instructive medley of quotations and classical anecdotes I ever perused* [italics, mine], but a superficial reader must take care or his (Burton's) intricacies will bewilder him.

Now, the fact is the book's title is misleading; it started out to be an exhaustive medical book, but it drifted into an extensive treatise upon all the things which might affect bodily and, more particularly, mental health. It passed through five editions in its author's lifetime; and, besides Byron, found favor with Charles Lamb, — who was much influenced by its author's quaintness, — Keats, Thackeray, and Sir William Osler, who took to Burton as I to Boswell. I make no doubt my friend Dr. Harvey Cushing is steeped in it. Burton was the psychoanalyst of his time, and the book is practically the life work of a shrewd old clergyman who enjoyed several ecclesiastical benefices, in which the work was done by curates and the pay taken by the incumbent, according to the good old fashion of the time. This gave its author an opportunity to become one of the most scholarly men in England, if not in the world. The book is compact with the wit and wisdom of the ancients and teems with extracts from classical authors, chiefly in Latin. It is divided into three "Partitions"; the last, — the longest and the most amusing, and for this reason the best known, — is called by its author, "Love Melancholy." It is one of the oldest diseases known, and its causes, manifestations, and cures are discussed with much pleasant naughtiness. One would suppose that by this time a panacea for the cure of love would have been discovered. But such does not appear to be the case, unless, as Burton — the cowardly old bachelor — rather more than hints, Possession will do the trick.

A good Burtonian (I fear I am too old to transfer my allegiance from Boswell) will require at least two copies of the *Anatomy:* the first edition (1621), of course; and, not less, the third edition (1628), the first with the engraved title, and its amusing and accompanying verses. This engraved title was used in several subsequent early editions. When I decided I wanted a copy of this edition in an old binding, I went to Dr. Rosenbach's, asked for it, and got it just as easy as easy. Lionel Robinson had a very fair copy of this edition the last time I was in his shop in Pall Mall, and a copy was offered me, only a few weeks ago, by Charles Sessler, the well-known bookseller of Philadelphia. Nevertheless the book is rare.

People talk about books for protracted stays on desert islands, of people one would wish to meet; for my part, were I in a choosy mood, I should wish that the two best Burtonians of my acquaintance, Paul Jordan-Smith of Hollywood, California, and Holbrook Jackson of London, might meet in my dining room, stretch their legs under my mahogany, and have their talk out. *Les extrêmes se touchent,* as the French so eloquently say. It may be that this will come about. I have a dining table well suited to the occasion; a silver plate let into it records the fact that

THIS TABLE AND THESE CHAIRS WERE FROM
1815 TO 1929 IN THE DINING ROOM OF
JOHN MURRAY'S RESIDENCE,
50 ALBEMARLE STREET, LONDON,
WHERE THE FAMOUS PUBLISHER CONSTANTLY
ENTERTAINED THE MOST DISTINGUISHED
LITERARY MEN OF HIS TIME.

BURTON'S "ANATOMY" AND ANOTHER

THE NAMES OF
BYRON, SCOTT, MOORE, SOUTHEY,
COLERIDGE, CAMPBELL, WASHINGTON IRVING,
AND MANY OTHERS CONSTANTLY COME TO MIND.
IT MAY BE THAT THEIR GHOSTS ARE OCCUPYING
THESE CHAIRS THIS VERY MINUTE.

X

LAURENCE STERNE

THE author of this book [1] is a very remarkable man; in proof of which I submit the following: He was, for many years, a Professor of English at Yale University; the author of many books, including *The History of Henry Fielding*, in three stout volumes; the author of *The Development of the English Novel*, which I have read several times and am constantly referring to; he retires on age from his professional activities and, to the amazement of his friends, throws himself into politics with the enthusiasm of a boy — and has himself elected, not once, but twice, Governor of the State of Connecticut. Englishmen sometimes abandon literature for politics, but over here it is most unusual. Politics is a game which only crooks are supposed to play with success. My friend Doctor,

[1] *The Life and Times of Laurence Sterne*, by Wilbur L. Cross, Yale University Press.

Professor, Governor Cross has met the enemy and they are his. "It seems strange," writes Dr. Cross to me, "that after completing my career I should go into politics." "Strange!" In my State it would be impossible. We in Pennsylvania have no use for a gentleman and a scholar, and we don't get them.

And now as to *The Life and Times of Laurence Sterne*. It was the chance observation of my friend Augustine Birrell that "If one reads for any better purpose than to waste time, the great thing is to keep pegging away at masterpieces in cheap editions," and the equally chance stumbling some years ago upon a copy of *The Life and Times of Laurence Sterne*, by Dr. Wilbur L. Cross, that led to my becoming a complete, if not a perfect, "Shandean." And whenever, in my library, I happened upon Dr. Cross's original volume, I always thought of how much pleasure it had given me, and promised myself the pleasure of reading it over again. When, therefore, a new edition of my old friend was announced, — I will not say "revised and corrected," for who would revise and correct an old friend? — in which was to be included many letters never before printed and reproductions of original manuscripts, I immediately placed an order with my bookseller for a copy; with the result that two excellently made volumes are now before me.

It is all that a book of this sort should be. If occasionally it is severe, no doubt Sterne deserved severity; but it is always sympathetic. And if the story of Sterne's life is told in great detail, the details only serve to enhance one's interest in the book. That it is the work of an accomplished scholar is obvious from the outset. And it turns into waste paper the English books on Sterne that have gone before — Fitzgerald's and Sichel's. (I own them and have read them.)

But, quite aside from the literary merit and skill of Dr. Cross, it was inevitable that this should be the case; for in recent years much unpublished material anent Sterne has come to America, most of it immediately finding its way into the Pierpont Morgan Library of New York, where it was at once made available to Dr. Cross. I plead in excuse for my own poor showing in Sterne the opposing fact that Mr. Morgan's collection is so rich; for who can stand against his wealth, intelligently directed as it is by Miss Belle da Costa Greene, the director of the library? I have all the first editions but only one letter and a scrap of the manuscript of *Tristram Shandy*.

Our author in his Introduction, also quoting Birrell, says: "Books do not live by comparisons but by their pleasure-giving qualities." This being the case, it is no rash thing to insure or assure a long life to the volumes now under consideration — for this is hardly a review. To be meticulously exact is the duty of a scholar, but it is only one of his duties; another, not less important, is that he should be readable, and this duty Dr. Cross has always kept clearly before him. No one interested in the "life and times" of the eighteenth century — and who is not? — can fail to find these volumes fascinating. Think of the leisure of the period and compare it with this century of bustle! Think of the joy of hiring a man for a cottage and sixteen pounds a year to do your job while you go off to the south of France for an indefinite stay!

END PAPERS

Some time ago, all on a summer's day, before these volumes appeared, I listened to a sermon delivered from the pulpit which Laurence Sterne — I hesitate to refer to him as "the Reverend" — occasionally adorned in the little church of St. Michael, picturesquely situated in the Coxwold Hills in Yorkshire, and after a pleasant chat with the rector tramped up the hill a short distance until I came to the rambling farmhouse in which the immortal *Tristram* was written. An amiable yeoman, seeing me pause to read the inscription cut into a stone slab over the entrance door, invited me to enter; but not before I had read: —

SHANDY HALL

HERE DWELT LAURENCE STERNE

MANY YEARS INCUMBENT

OF COXWOLD

HERE HE WROTE TRISTRAM SHANDY

AND THE SENTIMENTAL JOURNEY.

DIED IN LONDON IN 1768

AGED 55 YEARS

I was interested to see the tiny room in which the great book, and perhaps the lesser, was written; and looking around I thought of Sterne's "most religious way of beginning a book." "I write the first sentence — and trust to Almighty God for the second." I shall never again turn the pages of *Tristram* and read of my Uncle Toby, and Corporal Trim, and of the Abbess of Andoüillets, and of Margarita, of Le Fevre, and of the Widow Wadman, and of many other things, without thinking of that pleasant Sunday morning.

And the finest prose passage in the language, that paragraph about the recording angel, and that bit, "God tempers the wind to the shorn lamb," extracted from a deliciously naughty book, although some think it is taken from the Bible, were born in this tiny room! And to read in Dr. Cross of how this mortal put on immortality, and when and where, and sometimes why, is a delight — a sheer delight. Sterne died very much as he said he wanted to in *Tristram Shandy*, "not in his own house but rather in some decent inn away from the concern of his friends, where the few cold offices he required might be purchased for a few guineas." He had lodgings in Bond Street, London, very near to Sir Thomas Agnew's picture gallery — next door, I think. The house still stands, and there is a small tablet thereon: STERNE HOUSE. He was buried in the burial ground of the then — and now — fashionable St. George's Church, Hanover Square. And there is a pretty well-authenticated and gruesome story that his body was "resurrected" and found its way to a dissecting table in one of the colleges in Cambridge. Alas! Poor Yorick.

If this slender little paper leads any reader to renew his acquaintance with *Tristram Shandy*, he will feel indebted to me. And to one who has never read this classic I would say, "Take it slowly, a little at a time, and continue to read it until it *gets* you." It can, indeed it should, be skipped occasionally — but anyone skipping Dr. Cross's *Life and Times of Sterne* must have better acquired the art than I.

XI

JACK JORROCKS [1]

JACK JORROCKS is immortal. He is not only
witty (if we do not define wit too narrowly)
in himself, but the cause of wit in other men —
and thereby hangs a tale.

It is just one hundred years ago that a young
solicitor, Robert Smith Surtees, finding the
trade of soliciting not all that it was represented
to be, turned his attention to sporting matters
and, with the assistance of Rudolph Ackermann,
the well-known publisher, started the *New
Sporting Magazine* — there having been an old
Sporting Magazine which had gone the way
of all flesh and of most magazines of the period.
Robert Surtees was a gentleman, the second
son of Anthony Surtees of Hamsterley Hall,
near Durham, whose elder son died unmarried,
so that at his father's death Robert succeeded

[1] Introduction to *Jorrocks's Jaunts and Jollities*, published by the Limited Editions Club, and reprinted by
permission.

III

to the estate; but as the second son without expectations he came up to London, and while waiting for clients compiled *The Horseman's Manual, Being a treatise on the Soundness, the Law of Warranty and generally on the Laws relating to Horses* — a copy of which the writer, having no occasion whatever for its use, has had for many years in his collection of Sporting Books. It is a very scarce little volume, and, bearing in mind Anthony Trollope's observation that "not even a bishop can sell a horse without forgetting that he is a bishop," the book must at one time have had many readers; perhaps it has to-day. It was reprinted in New York the following year and this first American edition is, in all probability, rarer than the first English edition. This *Manual* is the only book on the title-page of which its author put his name. It begins, not by praising the craft of the law, — which too many lawyers affect to regard as a science (I regret that they have Gibbon's authority for so doing), — but in this manner: "The glorious uncertainty of the Law has long been proverbial." This promises well, and the promises are, I believe, well kept throughout. But the year 1831, which saw the birth of *The Horseman's Manual*, saw also the death of Robert's elder brother and a change in the condition of Robert himself. No longer was he expected to sit in chambers in Lincoln's Inn Fields awaiting clients: he had only to await the death of a father to come into a substantial estate. To pass the time pleasantly he threw himself into the editing of a *Sporting Magazine* and created Jack Jorrocks. Jorrocks, as my old friend Thomas Seccombe says in the *Dictionary of National Biography*, is a grocer of sporting proclivities: the quintessence of Cockney vulgarity, good humor, absurdity, and cunning. The doings of this renowned sporting citizen of St. Botolph Lane, where his place of business was, and of Great Coram Street, where, with his spouse, he resided, and more particularly his experiences afield and afloat, attracted a host of readers to the magazine. But publication in a magazine does not make for immortality: that comes only with publication in book form, between stiff covers; a book will hardly survive if "in parts" only, however much "parts" may be desired by the collector.

So *Jorrocks's Jaunts* was made to stand upright in 1838, with twelve illustrations by Phiz; also reprinted by Carey and Hart in Philadelphia that same year. But the "sought" edition is the "second," with fifteen hand-colored plates by Henry Alken, published in 1843 by Ackermann. It is a sort of treason to speak disrespectfully of Alken's illustrations, but these plates are certainly not Alken's best work.

Meantime, the success attending the Jorrocks sketches as originally published had led one Robert Seymour, an illustrator, to suggest to Messrs. Chapman and Hall the publication of a series of Cockney sporting plates; and they, while accepting the idea of the sketches, saw the desirability of "text" — *i.e.* reading matter — as well, and sent for Charles Dickens, then an obscure journalist. The rest is — not silence, but rather the reverse: everyone seems to have something to say. Out of the confusion certain facts emerge. Pickwick was born and lives forever. Dickens and Seymour quarreled, and Seymour shot himself. Another illustrator was found and failed; another, Thackeray, offered himself and was declined; then came H. K.

Browne (Phiz) and a certain measure of tranquillity. Pickwick is not, I think, in himself a much greater creation than Jorrocks; but, like many eminent men, he shines with the glory of others. Jorrocks has his "Binjamin," to be sure, but Pickwick has Sam Weller. But *Jorrocks came first*, and "not to know Jorrocks is indeed to argue oneself unknown."

If I have not made it clear that Surtees, the creator of Jorrocks, is a gentleman, the reader will, I hope, take an early opportunity of looking at a portrait of him made by the illustrator of this edition, Mr. Gordon Ross. He will see a man of great refinement, and will understand his wish that a distinction be drawn between describing vulgar people and describing vulgar people vulgarly. Jorrocks lived in a coarse age, but, as his legal representative observed during a trial scene which can hardly be matched for its humor, Mr. Jorrocks "was a gentleman who in all the relations of life, whether as a husband, fox hunter, shooter, or grocer, has invariably that character and reputation so valuable in commercial life, so necessary in the sporting world, so indispensable to a man moving in

general society." Anyone who picked Jorrocks
up for a fool, drunk or sober, dropped him
quickly; and I call attention to the incident
in which, at a dinner of the Surrey Foxhounds,
Mr. Juggins, the master of those same hounds,
announces much to Jorrocks's surprise that
famous sportsman's subscription of ten pounds
towards the support of the pack. Jorrocks,
having made no such offer, is for the moment
bewildered — but not for long. After the
cheering has subsided, he gets upon his feet
and, thanking his excellent friend "for the
werry flattening compliment in coupling his
name with the Surrey 'ounds," observes that
he "don't recollect saying nothing whatsomever
about it (*hiccup*), but being werry friendly to
sporting in all its ramifications (*hiccup*) will be
werry 'appy to give ten pounds to your 'ounds
provided my friend Juggins will give ten pounds
to ours!" A retort which may be very useful
these days, when one is constantly being be-
sieged to subscribe to the other man's charities.

Lockhart, Sir Walter Scott's son-in-law, is
credited with having made the suggestion that
the creator of Jorrocks try his hand at a novel.

Mr. Jorrocks Making His Famous Speech on Fox-'unting, the Sport of Kings

After a drawing by John Leech

Surtees did; the result was *Handley Cross*, in which Jorrocks reappears as the possessor of a county seat and a Master of Foxhounds, and this Jorrocks is the immortal figure. But in the sketches, in the *Jaunts and Jollities*, we see the material forming. We get the germ of his famous saying: "Fox-'unting is the sport of Kings, the himage of war without its guilt and only five and twenty per cent of its danger." We are told and believe that "to be surrounded by one's friends is the A-one of 'uman 'appiness," and while Jorrocks "leaves the flowers of speech to them as is acquainted with botany" he is able to express himself very neatly and to the point, except in France, where the language causes him much trouble — as it does me. And he was not impressed with French food. Since he is accustomed to a basin of good substantial soup, a plate of hot water "with worms" (macaroni) in it "causes his stomach to think that his throat is cut."

Mr. Jorrocks's description of a Channel crossing a hundred years ago is an amusing and, one feels, not exaggerated account of a voyage which even to-day, when it can be

abridged to a little more than an hour, still holds
the world in terror. It is the general belief
that more fish have been fed in that twenty
miles or so of much-traveled and tumbling sea
than in many times the distance elsewhere.
And the touts whose business it was to extol
the merits of their own boats and the mis-
behavior of their rivals' remind one of the mis-
creant hack drivers of Niagara Falls in the
early eighties — now, happily, a memory only.
But Jorrocks was equal to this occasion also.
"Gentlemen, gentlemen," said he, "your pur-
liteness knows no bounds, but to be candid with
you I beg to say that whoever will carry me
across the 'erring pond cheapest shall have my
custom, so now begin and *bid downwards*."
One is justified in believing that Mr. Jorrocks
did not secure passage in the *quickest* boat;
that he got what he paid for — as did the man
who declined to take gas at his dentist's, because
he wanted to feel that the said mechanic was
at work all the time that he was in the chair;
and he did.

Once again it is proven that humor, fun, wit —
call it what you will — is the best preservative

against the ravages of time. Dr. Johnson, in the preface to his edition of Shakespeare, says that one hundred years is the term commonly fixed as the test of literary merit. Jorrocks has stood this test and is still going strong.

A word must be said of this edition, and of its illustrator; but first, as a collector, one wishes to have, if one can afford it, the second edition, — the first with the Alken plates, — in order that one may enjoy especially the engraved and hand-colored title-page, which is one of the best ever made for a book. But not every lover of Jorrocks can afford or may care to spend the five hundred dollars or so necessary to secure a fine copy of the book in its original gray-green cloth. In that case, this is the edition to buy. Indeed, I shall be much surprised if all lovers of Jack Jorrocks will not want this edition also. Its merits are obvious: good paper, good printing, good binding: a good book to lie upon the window seat.

And now for Mr. Ross, his illustrations. No one now living in Great Britain and doing work in his line can compare with Gordon Ross, now living in New York. I shall not dare to call him an American: to do so would plunge this country into another war — with Scotland: it is well known how reluctant the Scot is to give up anything of value, and I cannot imagine anything which would reconcile them to the permanent loss of so excellent an artist as Gordon Ross. He has no living superior; I doubt if he has his equal for the very quality needed to illustrate a humorous classic. And if *Jorrocks's Jaunts and Jollities* be not a classic, then I know not where to look for one. A final word may be permitted. If this book sells as well as it should, I have a suggestion to make to its publishers. Why should they not get Mr. Ross to make illustrations for a new edition of *The Diverting History of John Gilpin?*

XII

THE CHRISTMAS SPIRIT

IT is an amusing world, my masters: laugh at it. Few are the customs so harmless that here or there, at one time or another, some silly priest or sinful politician has not risen up and cried, "Stop! In God's name, stop!" So if in an effort to keep wassail on Christmas Eve in this year of grace you have yourself drunk or served your friends liquor contrary to the spirit laws of the United States Government, or if you have, perchance, been arrested because the policeman on your beat has not been properly "seen," take comfort in the thought that it was once a crime to hang evergreens in your church, to light a candle, to sing a ballad, to do any one of half a hundred things the doing of which tends to make this old world of ours tolerable.

One Christmas Day, a small group of people were gathered in a certain place, when suddenly the building was surrounded and the company taken prisoners. Some were taken here, some there, and all subjected to great indignities. It sounds like a raid upon a night club, does it not? It was, however, only "authority" seeking to prevent some Christian people from worshiping God in Exeter Chapel, London, *on the 25th day of December in the year 1657*. The story can be read in the Diary of the unimpeachable John Evelyn. Far into the eighteenth century Presbyterian divines preached against the observance of Christmas, and as late as 1830 hymnbooks were in use in Baptist and other dissenting congregations which made no provision at all for, or reluctantly admitted, one or two poor hymns as suitable for the commemoration of the Nativity.

Now when Jesus was born in Bethlehem of Judæa in the days of Herod the King, a very interesting astronomical event happened; it will detain us only long enough to observe that if coming events cast their shadows before them, as they are said to do, these shadows do not enable us to fix with any certainty the year or the month or the day of the month when one of the greatest events in our world's history took place.

THE CHRISTMAS SPIRIT

I refer, of course, to the birth of Christ. The early Christians, to popularize this event, gave cherished pagan practices a twist, so that many of our Christmas customs date from the immemorial past. It was three hundred years or more after the event that the Church of Rome decided in her arbitrary way that the birth of Christ took place on the twenty-fifth day of December in the year Urbis Conditæ 753, or the seven hundred and fifty-third year of the building of the City of Rome, which later became Anno Domini I. And now, at last, we have the loveliest of legends nicely dated up with, finally, a wise Pope, Gregory I, permitting, and even suggesting, to Augustine of Canterbury that he encourage harmless popular customs and give them a Christian interpretation.

For some reason, beyond the ken of the writer, the Christmas Spirit never fully caught on in Italy or Spain or France. Germany and Holland and England, on the other hand, early took to Christmas: Santa Claus and Kriss Kringle, Saint Nicholas, and other forms of Father Christmas becoming popular in their respective countries. The Christmas tree habit is very old:

it comes from Egypt, via Germany; Luther developed it and made it the focal point of a Christmas celebration. The Prince Consort took the idea to England and there it was first seen in the great hall of Windsor Castle in 1841. How many millions of these trees are now growing in the forests of this country for use this Christmas, and next, and next after that, and so on!

But it remained for Charles Dickens, the greatest of all humanitarians, to take the Spirit of Christmas away from the priest, who had kept it all too long and done little good with it, and give it to the whole English-speaking world. When, in 1843, he published *A Christmas Carol*, he set ringing a chime of bells the sound of which is still heard around the world and throughout the year. People who have never heard of Charles Dickens have heard the tintinnabulation of his bells. Listen!

"Business," cries the Ghost, wringing its hands. "Mankind is my business. The common welfare is my business; charity, mercy, forbearance and benevolence are, all, my business. The dealings of my trade are but a drop of water in the comprehensive ocean of my business." There is the Christmas Spirit!

Bostonians tell us that Boston is not so much a place on the map as a state of mind. The same may be said of Christmas. We sing:—

> Christians, awake! Salute the happy morn,
> Whereon the Saviour of the world was born,

but we are thinking, "Have I forgotten anybody?" And this idea we owe to Charles Dickens. What a legacy to leave to the world! What preacher before, or since, has ever preached such a sermon! Well might Lord Jeffrey say, "The *Christmas Carol* has done more good than all the pulpits in Christendom." If some phantom should rise up before me as I pen these lines and say, "What is your wish? Shakespeare aside, what would you write if you could?" instantly I would reply, "Another and a better *Christmas Carol*," and at these words the apparition would, I am certain, fade away — I having outwished its power.

It is just ten years ago that I wrote for Ellery Sedgwick a slender introduction to an excellent facsimile reproduction of *A Christmas Carol*, published by the Atlantic Monthly Press. In it

I referred to the original manuscript of this lovely story, which is now in the Pierpont Morgan Library in the city of New York. Articles of greater value exist in that temple where scholars go to worship, but Miss Greene, the Librarian, tells me that at the exhibitions which are there held from time to time no item attracts greater attention than does the manuscript of the *Carol*. No one can see it without being the better for it. And, comparing small things with great, my library now contains not only a great group of *Carols*, in different "states," including several "presentation" copies given by Charles Dickens to his friends, but also the copy which once belonged to Charles Dickens himself and subsequently to Charles Plumptre Johnson, the Dickens collector, who wrote in his *Hints to Dickens Collectors:* "I have in my possession a copy *absolutely uncut*, which I believe to be the first copy printed and sent to the binder for his guidance." Since this copy passed into the "Oak Knoll" Library, I have had it carefully examined; and experts agree with me that it is a "pull" from the type before the forms were sent to the press. It is printed on heavy paper which has been wetted to get a good impression therefrom: the result is not unlike Braille, in reverse. The discovery of this copy has settled several very pretty bibliographical problems — and raised others, which need not be discussed here.

Upon a lower level than the *Carol*, upon a level as much lower as the Dead Sea is below a mountain peak, is the Christmas Card. It followed close upon the first appearance of the *Carol*. I am sometimes inclined to feel that we have not properly evaluated our own Washington Irving's influence upon what we have called the Christmas Spirit. I am not sufficiently familiar with the *Sketch Book* in numbers, — it is a bibliographical puzzle, — but in any event in 1820 Irving remarked: "Shorn as it is of its ancient and festive honors, Christmas is still a period of delightful excitement in England" — and thereupon proceeded charmingly to depict the hospitality and good cheer with which an "Old English Christmas" was celebrated. It was twenty-three years later that the *Carol* appeared. It started the giving habit; but the *Carol* cost money, five shillings originally; then someone had the bright idea — perhaps it was

Raphael Tuck, the publisher, himself — of getting out a Christmas Card. In 1845, two years after the *Carol*, came the Card. It was designed by J. C. Horsley, R.A., and was printed or lithographed in one color, dark brown, and painted by hand somewhat in the same manner as the illustrations in the first and early editions of *A Christmas Carol*. The picture resolves itself into three panels, the centre one representing a family group of three generations indulging in the Christmas Spirit. Let us look upon this picture while we can: it may soon be declared a crime even to look upon a scene so degrading. The designs of the side panels suggest the clothing of the naked and the feeding of the hungry.

The popularity of this, the first Christmas Card, was not very great: the idea was slow of acceptance and one would have been declared mad had one suggested that in a few years millions, and in later years hundreds of millions, of cards — many of them works of art — would flood the mails at this season.

I secured the original card, the only one I have ever seen, a year or two ago in London, thinking that I might one day use it as a means of conveying to my friends the Spirit of Christmas.

When this little paper was originally printed and circulated, privately, three years ago, it looked as though that awful curse called "prohibition" had been fastened on us indefinitely. The Honorable James M. Beck, who represents a thankless Philadelphia in Congress, after making one of the finest speeches made in Washington in this generation, urging the repeal of the prohibition amendment, told me that it was hopeless to expect anything to come of the efforts of the anti-prohibitionists for a generation. Three years later its overthrow is assured. It is amazing that honest and well-meaning men and women found it possible to strike hands with the thugs and bootleggers, who for many years throve upon the illegal liquor traffic. Prohibition, as I see it, has not only cost us billions in money; it has lowered the moral tone of every man, woman, and child in the nation. It brought in its wake disregard and disrespect for all law. Its cost in mere money was its least cost. Men lived "wet," voted "dry," and were unashamed. It confirmed hypocrites in their hypocrisy. I once dined at the house of a governor of an important state. The dinner was excellent; especially good were the wines. The next day I was disgusted to see this same governor come out with what the newspapers called "A Clarion Cry for Prohibition."

But it is over. We shall take the liquor question out of the Constitution, where it had no right to be, and put it into our police regulations, and then devote ourselves to a further reform — the reform of our police. We have subjected them to a test quite as cruel as that which in Ireland was, at one time, designed to try the virtue of young acolytes who were being prepared for holy orders. The story will be found in George Moore's *A Storyteller's Holiday*. I believe that " Al " Smith has more to do with lifting from our shoulders the curse of prohibition than any other man. I honor him and regret that I did not vote for him; just as I believe that the cowardly vacillation of Mr. Hoover, "the forgotten man," whom I did vote for, was very largely responsible for its long and unnecessary continuance.

XIII

AGNES REPPLIER — OUR BEST BLUESTOCKING

WOULD that we had a pair; but her color is hard to match. There is, I think, no one, man or woman, in England or America, who is quite in her class. She is possessed of the whole bag of tricks of the complete essayist: knowledge, humor, irony, sarcasm (in full measure — God direct it not my way!), wide reading, an inexhaustible memory; anything more? Yes, a certain authority and maturity which one associates with old Montaigne, the father of her art. But that the essay as a literary form has fallen on parlous times, her name would be sounded in all the churches. I leave the lady on the knees of Father Time, who will know how to deal with her, albeit such ladies are unusual in his experience.

There was a time when Philadelphia was an important literary and publishing centre; but it has fallen, and fallen hard. College professors we have in abundance, but I have not now college professors in mind, not even the doyen of his profession, my honored old friend, Felix Schelling. I am thinking of an older generation; men like Charles Brockden Brown, Thomas Montgomery Bird, and George H. Boker. In Agnes Repplier we have one who carries on with equal distinction a fine literary tradition. For many years she has been supporting herself, nobly, by her pen, and I am glad of an opportunity of declaring myself her disciple. If Miss Repplier had lived anywhere but in the City of Brotherly Love she would be recognized for what she is, a national figure. But we Philadelphians are a queer lot, "corrupt and contented," as Lincoln Steffens has said, but in this we are not singular: our singularity consists in the extremity to which we have carried the Chinese custom of ancestor worship; with the result that to make one's mark in Philadelphia one has to leave home. This Miss Repplier has not done; she has always been a Philadelphian.

It is just a year ago that she published a new book of essays, *To Think of Tea*. I instantly bought a copy, and as I read it coming home in the train an idea came to me. "Here is an opportunity," I said, "to stimulate the sale of a good book"; and immediately upon reaching my desk I hurriedly penned the following: —

My friend Agnes Repplier's new book, *To Think of Tea,* is a sheer delight. It is compact with learning, and wisdom, — which is not the same thing, — and it is ironical and witty. I am pleased to note that as the lady grows older (she is no longer in her thirties) she, like Dr. Johnson, "is 'prepared to call a man a good man on easier terms than heretofore.'" The format of the book is admirable. It is published by Houghton Mifflin Co. of Boston, and costs $2.75. I regret that, times being what they are, I cannot afford to send you a copy. But I 'll tell you what I will do. If you buy a copy and don't like it I will take it off your hands for $1.50 and give it to some appreciative friend at Christmas. Thus it will cost you only $1.25 to read one of the most delightful volumes of essays that has appeared in years.

I did not wait for a proof: I had several hundred cards printed, turned them over to my secretary with my mailing list, and within a few hours they were in the post.

I hoped that I had started something and warned several bookshops in Philadelphia of what was likely to happen; but they were hardly prepared for the orders that they received, nor were the publishers, when they found orders pouring in from all over the country. In less than a month the first edition of three thousand copies had been disposed of and an edition was printing in London. "Good wine needs no bush" — maybe not, but the personal indorsement of a good book does no harm.

Then it was suggested "Why not give Agnes Repplier a tea party?" and in due course we sat down forty at table, which is the capacity of our best dining room. A part of the festivities was to include the reading of some extracts from her book, but we never got round to that. Friends and neighbors, hearing that something was going on, surged in upon us; and Miss Repplier was kept busy pouring tea for all and sundry from my only relic, Dr. Johnson's teapot. Seated in my library, under a Reynolds portrait of Johnson, with Charlie Osgood, the English scholar of Princeton, standing by, we had her photograph taken as a record of the occasion. I take pleasure in reproducing it.

It was just before Christmas and the weather was abominable; but not a single guest failed

To Think of Tea

In the library at "Oak Knoll" — Miss Repplier pouring, Mr. Charles G. Osgood standing, Mr. and Mrs. Newton

us.   As night came on and rain turned to sleet
and snow, the motors of our departing guests
skidded as though on glass, and wind shields
became as opaque as a snowdrift.   Have you
gathered from my encomiums that Agnes Repplier is without fault or blemish?   I would conceal them if I could, but truth compels me to
state that she has at least two.   She will look
at first editions of famous books with the same
lack of interest that I feel and try to conceal
when shown a collection of postage stamps.
And she hates the country; she prefers the sights
and noise and smells of the city.   For this, I
regret that she has Charles Lamb's authority.
As I handed her into her motor, she turned to
me and witheringly remarked, "And you prefer this to the city!"   The next morning I said
to my outside man, "Did you have much trouble
with the cars yesterday?"   "No, sir, not much,"
was the reply, "the trouble was had by them in
the motors.   Their cars slipped aroun' somethin'
dreadful and they made havick of my flower beds
— but it will all be forgot by spring."   For real
philosophy eschew the college Ph.D. and con-
sult the colored brother.

A few weeks later I was lunching with my old
friend Augustine Birrell at the Garrick Club in
London.   We spoke of Miss Repplier, — whom
he insisted on calling Mrs. Repplier, — he was
enthusiastic about her book, and told me he had
written a review for the *Observer*.   I got a copy.
He gave her a full column of praise, but, characteristically, closed in this manner: —

Our space is exhausted.   A critic must find fault
and our authoress has one which, like her subject,
is so akin to virtue that we are almost ashamed to
mention it.   Mrs. Repplier has a marvelous gift for
apt quotation from other writers, and an apt quotation is as refreshing as an ill-timed one is repulsive.
But she deems it her duty to name the author from
whom she quotes, and somehow or another this over-
loads her sprightly page.   It is quite unnecessary.
This is an Age of Scribblers, and we all live by taking
in each other's washing; there is, however, no need
to give the name of the laundress!

I think of a bookcase, not a small one, which
contains my favorite volumes of essays — essays
old and new.   I think of Lamb and Hazlitt, and
of Alexander Smith's *Dreamthorp;* of Lang and
Dobson; and, above all, of that series which
began half a century ago with *Obiter Dicta*.

Barring Lamb, at whose shrine I worship, are any of them better than Agnes Repplier's? Hardly. Her work is as aromatic as spice. I have in mind one special little volume, *A Happy Half Century*, published many years ago. The happy half century was from 1775 to 1825, when anyone — particularly any woman — could assure herself of immortality, according to her friends, merely by smearing ink upon paper. And, in this volume, an essay entitled "The Literary Lady" I have read a score of times. It gives Miss Repplier such scope and margin for her acidulated fun that one cannot escape the feeling that Anna Seward and Hannah More, Mrs. Trimmer, Mrs. Montague, and the rest were created for this especial purpose.

"Do you collect Agnes Repplier?" a scholarly bookseller in London once asked me.

"Certainly I do," I replied. "Why?"

"Because, to my mind, she is the best essayist writing in English to-day."

I am glad to have my opinion confirmed by such an authority as Mr. A. W. Evans of the firm of Elkin Mathews and Company.

XIV

PROLEGOMENON TO A BOOKSELLER'S CATALOGUE

My young friend, Hugh Tregaskis, asked me
to write an introduction to a book catalogue
to be issued by his firm. I could not deny
myself the pleasure of complying with his
request; but there was, as always, a fly in the
amber. It made me feel very old when I
found myself thinking of Hugh as he was when
I first met him, twenty-three years ago. He
was then a precocious lad of six years, the apple
of his father's eye, and my old friend, his father,
whom I knew well and used to call "Jimmy,"
was fortunate in living long enough to see this
same lad grow into a man, and to take him into
his business, wherein he promised to add lustre
to the name of Tregaskis.

James Tregaskis came of an old Cornish
family, and was proud of it. There is a saying
down in Virginia, "Never ask a man where he
comes from. If he was born in Virginia, sooner

or later he will tell you so; if he was not, that is no reason why he should be humiliated." In my ignorance, many years ago, I once asked Jimmy Tregaskis in what part of England he was born. I say I *once* asked him: I had no occasion to ask him a second time; he made it perfectly clear that he was a Cornishman. He was born in the little hamlet of St. Day on April 23, 1850. Twenty years later he came to London to enter Blenkinsop and Co., his uncle's printing business, and nine years later he became a partner therein. In the meantime there had been established in Birmingham, by one Robert Wilde, a book business which issued catalogues as from the Caxton Head. The first of these was dated 1874. In 1881 the business was purchased by W. P. Bennett, who, four years later, in June 1885, transferred it to London, where he occupied premises at 39, Great Russell Street. The first catalogue issued from this address describes a First Folio of Shakespeare, lacking the preliminary leaves, but bound by Roger Payne, priced at sixty-five guineas! Bennett died in due course and his widow, Mary Lee Bennett, succeeded to the business, which she subsequently transferred to 232, High Holborn. While at this address Mrs. Bennett met and subsequently married James Tregaskis, who was still in the printing business; but notebooks which date as far back as 1883 show his deep interest in old books, so it is not surprising that he finally exchanged the business of printer for that of bookseller, and in February 1890 we find catalogues in which his name appears in conjunction with that of his wife, formerly Mrs. Bennett.

In March 1891 Tregaskis, always interested in fine bindings, announced a European Book-binding Exhibition, which occasioned much favorable comment; and later, in 1894, he launched a more ambitious plan in the form of an International Bindings Exhibition. In this he displayed seventy-five copies of the Kelmscott edition of *King Florus and the Fair Jehane*, each copy bound by one of the leading binders of the world. This was indeed enterprise, not too frequently shown by antiquarian book-sellers. The newspapers devoted much space to the Exhibition, and Tregaskis was soon in receipt of a royal summons to Windsor, Queen

Victoria having expressed the wish to see the collection. After this most unusual mark of royal approval, Tregaskis took his proper place as one of the most important booksellers in Great Britain. He very wisely declined to break up the collection, and subsequently sold it *en bloc* to Mrs. John Rylands; and it is now preserved in the famous John Rylands Library in Manchester.

In 1900 Mrs. Tregaskis died, and her husband, inheriting the business, changed the firm name to James Tregaskis merely, quaintly adding to his address (232, High Holborn): "in the Parish of St. Giles-in-the-Field, London." In those days good tradesmen frequently lived over their shops, and I remember having seen a charming drawing, by Herbert Railton, of a fine old-time staircase leading to the upper floors of the premises occupied by Mr. Tregaskis and his family. Three years after the death of the first Mrs. Tregaskis, Mr. Tregaskis married Eveline Belwood Davis, by whom he had a son, born in 1905, christened Hugh. When the lease of the old building in High Holborn fell in, Tregaskis purchased a charming freehold property for himself and his family in Hampstead, removing the business in March 1915 to its present location, 66, Great Russell Street, opposite the British Museum, which he frequently referred to as his reference library.

I came to know Tregaskis well while he was still in Holborn, and I have before me as I write Catalogue No. 723, published April 22, 1912, containing "A List of Rare and Interesting Books, comprising a Collection of Works by and relative to Dr. Johnson and some other famous English Writers of the Eighteenth Century." Tregaskis was himself an ardent Johnsonian, and from the Caxton Head came many of my finest Johnson items. For my *London,* in contemporary boards, I paid the now trifling sum of seven pounds, and my copy of Boswell's *Tour to the Hebrides,* "Presented to James Boswell Esquire, Junior, from his Affectionate Father the Authour," cost only thirty-eight! Those were the days! And I am not, I think, mistaken in saying that it was to Tregaskis that I owe my first introduction to the Johnson Club, of which I subsequently became an honorary member and of which he was at one time Prior.

This may be as good a time as any to say that if James Tregaskis was a shrewd and foresighted merchant, I ever and always found him to be a frank, generous and kindly host, and I shall never forget the many pleasant hours we spent together.   Talk with a good bookseller can hardly be bettered, as all collectors know, and when I learned that my old friend Tregaskis had passed away on November 23rd, 1926, I felt that one of the many magnets which drew me annually to London was gone — never to be replaced.

Since his death the Caxton Head is responsible for the publication of three books.   The first of these, a facsimile of the first English type-specimen book, was published in 1928.   This was followed by a facsimile of the catalogue of Sterne's library, and this year a more important publication has been completed in the form of Tusser's *Five Hundred Points of Good Husbandry* with a benediction by Rudyard Kipling and an introduction by E. V. Lucas.

The present shadows which have fallen across all business enterprise will pass.   At a time when money values are changing almost from hour to hour, good books afford a solace, and a safer investment than most; hence I venture the prophecy that when the Caxton Head shall publish its fifteen-hundredth catalogue some collector of the future will look upon the items and prices in this catalogue with the same longing that I now look back upon the one published by the elder Tregaskis, twenty years ago. Of the making of many books there is no end. True. But not of Caxton Head books.

XV

A STEVENSON MEMENTO

In the month of November, 1914, there was exhibited at the Grolier Club in New York City a collection of first editions of the works of Robert Louis Stevenson, together with some small but choice examples of Stevensoniana. Item No. 250 of this exhibition was a tiny blank book in which Stevenson, as a child of six, wrote his Bible lessons and texts in large printed characters. It is aptly described as a "Text Book," signed "R. L. B. S. 1856," and it is obviously a manuscript of Stevenson's earliest childhood. But it is not the first work of his genius or imagination : it is the first work of his hand, but not of his mind.

By the chance of the auction room I was recently fortunate enough to secure through Gabriel Wells, the bookseller of New York, the original draft of what seems to be Stevenson's earliest literary composition, dictated by him at the age of six, in the handwriting of his mother. The story of the manuscript of Stevenson's first book will be interesting to all lovers of Stevenson, — and who is not? — and may here be briefly told.

In 1856 Stevenson's Uncle David offered to his children and nephews a prize for the best history of Moses. Louis, then a child of only six years, was allowed to try for it, by dictating his version to his mother, and to this he devoted five successive Sunday evenings. He won the prize, and, adds his mother, "From that time it was the desire of his heart to be an author."

Stevenson himself in later years attributed much of his desire for writing to the childhood stories told him by his nurse, Alison Cunningham, and to her reading to him "the works of others as a poet would scarce dare to read his own."

In the volume of notes on Stevenson kept by his mother, she makes the following entry regarding the manuscript: —

It was begun on Nov. 23d and finished Dec. 21st; he dictated every word himself on the Sunday evenings — the only help I gave him was occasionally to read aloud to him from the Bible to refresh his memory.

This manuscript is signed by him "R. L. B. Stevenson," the B. standing for Balfour; he was christened Robert Lewis Balfour. In addition to the manuscript of twenty-three pages, there are eight pages of pencil sketches colored in water colors, entirely, in design and execution, the work of the boy himself.

When it is remembered that the drawings with their colorings, and the text, although in the handwriting of his mother, are the thought of the child expressed in his own words, it will be realized that this unique memento of Stevenson's childhood days cannot fail to appeal, not only to all Stevenson collectors, but to all who feel an interest in the earliest manifestation of genius. It will be observed that the spelling of the name as it appears in the inscription is Lewis; later he changed the spelling to Louis. The pronunciation of the word has always been the same.

Accompanying the manuscript as it came to me is the *Bible Picture Book* presented to Stevenson as the prize for his successful effort. An inscription in his uncle's handwriting reads: "R. Lewis B. Stevenson. A Reward for his History of Moses, with illustrations. From his affect. Uncle David, Christmas 1856."

HISTORY OF MOSES

There was a woman that had a child when all the babies were to be drowned and she was a good woman and she asked God how she could save her baby and God told her to make a basket of rushes and put it in the water hiding it in the rushes. Then Pharaoh's daughter was going to bathe in a certain place and as she went past she saw the cradle and asked her servants to go and bring it out and they did it. When they brought it out they lifted the thing up that was on the top and they saw a baby crying. Then they saw the child's sister that was standing far away and Pharaoh's daughter cried to her to come and when she came she told her to call a nurse for the baby and then she ran and brought the mother of it and she told the mother to take charge of it and to come to the palace and so she came.

Then Moses when he was grown up was sent

away to show some wonders to the Israelites
and God told him the things he was to do. He
first told him to lay down his rod and when he
laid it down it became a serpent. Then he told
him to go and do it when he was with the Israelites and he said he would do it. Then God told
him to put his hand into his breast and he did so
and his hand became a leper, then he pulled it
out and he put it in again and when he pulled
it out it was just the way it was before. Then
God told him to do that and he went away
home to the house that he lived in and God told
him that he would have to go to the Israelites.
Then he went away to the Israelites.

One day Moses saw a Egyptian whipping a
Israelite and he came and killed the Egyptian.
It was not wrong of Moses to kill the Egyptian
because he was doing harm to the Israelite for
he was an Israelite too. After that God told
Aaron and Moses to go up and try to make
Pharaoh let the Israelites go away and then
Aaron and Moses went up to speak to him and
asked him if he would allow them to go and Pharaoh said no that he would n't. Then Aaron laid
down the rod and behold it became a serpent.

He took it by the tail and pulled it up and it turned into a rod. He put his hand into his breast and it became a leper and he put it in again and it was just as it was before. Then the Egyptians took all their rods and laid them down and they became serpents. Pharaoh said he would let them go but he hardened his heart and would not. When Pharaoh was going to bathe at a certain place Aaron stretched his rod over the water and it became blood. Then Pharaoh went home in despair and he said he would let them go but he hardened his heart again. Then Aaron stretched out his rod and frogs came forth and crept over all the beds and eat up all the food and everything and he said he would let them go but he hardened his heart again.

Then the next plague was little insects called lice which went all over the country. After that he sent swarms of flies which buzzed about in the most horrible manner. Then boils came all over the people even over Pharaoh and his servants. After that came deaths of beasts and nearly all the beasts died. Then God sent hail and rain and fire and thunder and before he sent it he told Pharaoh and all his people to keep in their houses. After that it happened all the grass was taken away and all the leaves off the trees by locusts. Then it turned all darkness and it was all light beside the Israelites. And God said to the Israelites that they must all get ready and stand round a table eating a lamb and spread the blood of the lamb on the lintels of their doors for that the angel of death was going to pass to kill all the babies but who-ever has the blood on the lintels would n't have their babies killed. Then when the Egyptians had gone to bed thinking of no danger, the angel of death passed through and every baby even Pharaoh's first born was killed and there was a great cry over all the land. Then Pharaoh cried for Moses and Aaron as quickly as possible and he said that they must go away as fast as they could and they all went and took their bags of meat and their flocks and they asked the women of Egypt to give them some gold and silver and they did so.

They came to a sea called the Red Sea, now don't suppose it was red like blood, so the black cloud stood still that had led them all the way and they encamped and soon they heard a great noise of horses and chariots and it was the Egyptians coming after them. They then told Moses to go and pray to God and he did so. Then God told Moses to stretch out his rod over the Red Sea and he did so. Lo and behold the waters went up on each side of a dry path like walls, then the Israelites went into the path to cross. After they had got a little way across the Egyptians came up and they saw a dry path and they determined to go over it. They had not got very far across when lo and behold to their terror the wheels of their chariots stuck like as if in mud as God poured down his wrath and the thunder roared and such lightnings as were never seen in Egypt. Then God told Moses to stretch his rod over the water and he did so and the walls of water came down upon the tops of the Egyptians and they were drowned.

Then the Israelites were very hungry and they began to speak to Moses about it. Then Moses prayed to God and God told Moses that the Israelites were to get up very early in the morning and they would see small white things on the ground and they were to gather it but they were not to gather any for to-morrow because it would breed worms and stink and they could not eat it but on Saturdays they were to gather some for Sundays because on Sundays they would not see any little white things. So they rose up early in the morning and they went out and they did see little white things and they called it manna. It tasted like honey. Then they were very thirsty and they murmured against Moses and against God and so Moses went to pray to God and God told Moses to go up to a rock with a few men and to strike the rock with his rod and water would come out, so he did so and water came flowing forth. Then they traveled on through the wilderness and they came to a mount called Sinai. God told Moses to come up to him in the mount and Moses went up. God told Moses that he was to tell the Israelites to wash their clothes for they were to hear him speaking on the third day. They did so and on the third morning they heard his voice and the trumpet sounded loud. And he was to put railings round the mountain and he was not to let any of the people touch the mountain or the railings.

Moses stayed forty days and forty nights with God and God gave him two tables of stone with ten commandments written on them and the Israelites thought the time so long they thought he was never to come back so they asked Aaron to make them a golden calf. He told them to give all their gold earrings and things so he melted them and took it out and when it was soft he cut it into the shape of a calf. Then he took it and put it upon a high place and he said they should have a great feast to-morrow and so they had a grand feast and they danced round the calf and cried, "This is the one who brought us out of Egypt" and Moses was coming down at that time and he saw the Israelites dancing round the image and he broke the tables of stone because he was so angry and he came down very quickly and took the calf and melted it and ground it into powder and threw it into some water and made them drink it and God said that somebody must take a sword and kill some of them and Moses asked God not to kill the whole of them and said, "Remember what you promised to Jacob."

Then Moses went up into the mount again

154

and God told him to make a tabernacle and he
told him of two clever men which could help
them to carve wood and things. Their names
were Bezaleel and Aholiab. When Moses went
down they could not look upon him because
he shone with the glory of God and he put a
veil over his face. Then he told the Israelites
that they were to make a tabernacle for God and
Moses asked them for their gold and silver and
all their beautiful things to make it of and they
gave them. In the court of the tabernacle,
there was a brazen altar for offering lambs
and oxes upon and there was a brazen basin a
little farther in, in which the priests used to wash
the dishes and their hands. Then in the inside
in the holy place there was a golden altar for
burning incense on and a candlestick which had
seven lamps upon it. Then draw up the veil of
the tabernacle, you will see the Holy of Holies
and in it a large box of gold, the top of it was
called the Mercy Seat and there was two gold
angels that bent their wings over the top, in the
inside there was Aaron's budding rod and the
tables of stone. The Holy of Holies was a light
place because the glory of God was in it.

After the Israelites left Mount Sinai they came to a place near Canaan and they sent twelve men to see what like it was. When they had come into it they saw a great vine and so they plucked a bunch of grapes and one man could not carry it so they took a long staff and tied the grapes to it and Caleb and Joshua carried it and the rest carried figs and pomegranates. Then when they came to the Israelites they asked what kind of place it was and they said that the cities had strong gates and walls and that the people were giants and they were just like grasshoppers beside them. Then the Israelites said no, they would never conquer them. Then Caleb and Joshua struck up and said yes they would for God would help them for the people in Canaan only worshiped images. But the people did not believe Caleb and Joshua and sat up all night moaning and crying. Then God was angry and said they would never come into Canaan but were to wander forty years in the wilderness, but their children when they grew up were to go into Canaan and Caleb and Joshua were to go. They traveled away from that place back into the wilderness, then they murmured and said to Moses "Why did you bring us out of Egypt? Here we have neither water nor food." Then Moses prayed to God and God told him to take his rod and speak to the rock. Then Moses went away and took his rod and Aaron came with Moses and they said, "Here now ye rebels must we bring you water out of this rock," and Moses struck the rock with his rod and water came flowing forth and God said to Moses and Aaron that they should not go into Canaan but should die and Moses prayed to God and asked him if he might go into it and God told him not to pray any more because he should not go into it but God said to Moses that he should not die so soon as Aaron.

Then when they came to a place in the wilderness there was a great lot of serpents and their mouths burned like fire and God sent them among them when they murmured and they bit them and it made them very ill and they said to Moses to pray to God that he might take away the serpents from them. Then God told Moses to take some brass and soften it in the fire and to cut it into the shape of one of the serpents and to put it upon a pole and to hold up the pole and the Israelites who looked at the serpent would get better. That should put us in mind of Jesus, because the old serpent the Devil bit us, that means made us naughty and when we look at Jesus that makes us better — not to look at Jesus with our eyes but to look with praying. Then God took away the serpents and when the Israelites looked at the brazen serpent they were quite well.

Then God said to Moses that he would have to die and God sent Moses alone up to a high hill called Nebo where he could see the whole land of Canaan and God buried him in a valley in the land of Moab and nobody knows where Moses was buried to this day. And there was great weeping in all Israel for Moses.

RL B-stevenson.

Facsimile of R. L. S.'s Early Signature.

XVI

I WANT! I WANT!

THE son of a friend of mine, a lad of eight, upon being asked what he wanted to be when he grew up, having in mind his father's satisfaction in devoting his days to sport and his nights to cards, replied: "I think I should like to be a retired business man." Now, although I have no liking for sport and know not one card from another, I applaud his choice. Why should I not, having just made that election myself?

During my life I have changed my wants several times, but the time approaches when I must settle on something and stick to it. Time was when I wanted to be an angel!

> I want to be an angel
> And with the angels stand,
> A crown upon my forehead —
> A harp within my hand.

How often have I joined in singing this old-time catch! But I have given that over, the more curiously as I shall soon be coffin-ripe, the next state to which is being an angel. Decidedly I have now no wish to be an angel, and my friends assure me there is little chance of it.

If the reader of this little paper will turn to the accompanying illustration, he will see an enlargement of an engraving by William Blake. The original appears in a very tiny and excessively rare little booklet which rejoices in two titles: one is *For the Sexes*, the other, *The Gates of Paradise*. The original engraving is very small, measuring only one and five-eighths by two and three-eighths inches. May I say that it does not represent what you think it does. It does not represent a man climbing up to the moon, *sic itur ad astra*, but quite the reverse. It shows a man coming down to earth, a journey which most of us have recently completed. Our position is now much safer than it was; if we fall now it will not hurt us much.

"There is always room at the top," they say, but many who have reached an exalted position have found it very uncomfortable. I suspected as much; and, long before I reached it, decided to climb down as soon as I conveniently could.

I WANT! I WANT!

After an engraving by William Blake

I WANT! I WANT!

The small figure on the ladder may, then, be considered a portrait of the writer seeking a position of safety.

Regaining the earth from which I started more than fifty years ago, I looked about me to see what I should like to do with my hard and recently won leisure. This question of leisure is a difficult one; we have not been trained to it, and most of us do not take to it kindly. I see much in the papers about the five-day week and the six-hour day, but I have yet to read anything about highly paid executives who have accumulated more money than they can wisely spend retiring from the business trough in order that some younger and probably more capable fellow may get a chance at it. They affect to feel that their places cannot be taken, that "they have duties to perform to their stockholders!" Don't laugh. Our "Captains of Industry," of whom we once heard so much, deserve to be reduced to the ranks. Instead of which, the late Mr. Hoover sends for them, — the bankers and the business men, who, with the help of Congress, pretty damn near wrecked the country, — and asks them to suggest a way out of the difficulties they have created. Their suggestion is a shorter day and less wages for labor, not a shorter year for themselves. *La morale est toujours pour les autres.*

In this frame of mind, I decided to capitalize some of the honorary degrees I have received and become a college professor; and I was furthered in this notion by visits to my friends: Osgood, of Princeton, pleasantly summering in Woodstock, *Vermont* (he having invited me to come to him in Woodstock, New Hampshire!); Schelling, of Pennsylvania, turned farmer for the nonce (I don't know how long a nonce is, but he is the owner of a tithe barn big enough to hold a tenth of everything grown in his county), and Tinker, of Yale. I cannot expect the gods to be as good to me as to them, but if the luxury in which they live is general among college professors, and I am assured that it is, I ask nothing better.

And I was confirmed in this decision by an experience I had a few evenings ago.

The house was quiet, my wife had gone to bed, and I was just debating whether I should turn in or light a fresh cigar, when the 'phone rang.

I answered it, and heard a nervous and unknown voice saying, "You don't know me, Mr. Newton" — and then a pause.

This gave me an opportunity of saying, nastily, "Well, if all the people I don't know call me on the telephone, I shall have a sleepless night."

"Yes, I know," was the reply, "but I want to ask you a question."

"Well, do you mind asking it?"

"You know all about Dr. Johnson. What was the name of his cat? Someone asked me and I did n't know, but I said you would and that 's the reason I 've called you up."

(College professors ask and answer lots of silly questions like this.)

"Madam," I said (I was talking to a woman), "the name of Dr. Johnson's cat was Hodge. Johnson said that Hodge was a fine cat, but that he had a cat that he liked better, and then, as though perceiving Hodge's feelings were hurt, added, 'But Hodge is a very fine cat.' Now the question you should have asked me, as an authority, is: 'What was the name of Dr. Johnson's *other* cat?' Every schoolboy knows of Hodge, but the name of Johnson's other cat —

that is known only to the college professors, to people who are privileged to put initials after their names and wear Phi Beta Kappa keys."

"Are you so privileged?"

"I am."

"Do you know the name of Dr. Johnson's other cat?"

"I do."

"What was it?"

"Madam, that is a profound secret. I will let you into it only so far as to say that Dr. Johnson's other cat was a lady and 'well behaved.' I can tell you no more without permission from my Chapter." Here I said "Good night," and hung up the 'phone.

I wonder how many good Johnsonians know the name of Dr. Johnson's other cat?

But after all, I have decided upon being a lawyer.

> I want to be a lawyer
> And with the lawyers stand,
> A wig upon my forehead —
> A big fee in my hand.

I don't want to be a practising lawyer; I prefer to be a sentencing one. I have long had the idea that a judge's life was a very enviable one, and I was confirmed in this belief by a remark once made to me by that eminent jurist, Ellis Ames Ballard (an eminent jurist is one who is especially gifted in making twelve men believe that the worse is the better cause), who once said to me: "It is very easy to be a good judge. Give your opinion, but do not give your reason — if you do, your reason will reverse your opinion; give your opinion briefly, and go home."

And so it was that a few months ago, when Sir Henry Fielding Dickens, the only surviving son of our greatest novelist, asked me if I had had any judicial experience, I took a chance and told him I had "concurred" in a famous decision rendered by a Supreme Court judge in the state of California. A man had sued for damages sustained in falling into a coal hole. The lower court, finding that the plaintiff had been intoxicated at the time of the accident, decided that he had no case. Thereupon the plaintiff took the case to the upper court. The decision was, "If the defendant was at fault in leaving an uncovered hole in the sidewalk of a public street, the intoxication of the plaintiff cannot excuse such gross negligence. A drunken man is as much entitled to a safe street as a sober one, and much more in need of it. The judgment is reversed." *Newton concurring.*

"Excellent," said Sir Henry. Thereupon he asked me if I would not help him the next day at the Old Bailey, and I agreed to do so. "Very well," said Sir Henry, "You meet me at a few minutes past ten at the Sheriff's Entrance to the Old Bailey. I shall be glad of your help."

I was punctual to the stroke of ten, and after a brief delay was ushered into a court room, took my place in a great armchair, and began to look about me. The court room was crowded. On the desk in front of me, on the carpet, and wherever they could be lodged was a scattering of herbs, a custom introduced centuries ago to sweeten the air and reduce the chance of "gaol fever" (Cardinal Wolsey, in Shakespeare's *Henry the Eighth*, always carries an orange for the same reason). Presently Sir Henry entered, his horsehair wig hardly serving to give one of the most humane of men a ferocious aspect. His Worship carried a small bouquet of fresh flowers;

this, with the scattered herbs, gave a sweet and fragrant atmosphere to the whole place. But there was another atmosphere, even more important than the one occasioned by the herbs and flowers, which is never absent from an English court room — an atmosphere of justice and dignity, which is sadly lacking at our trials. I have seen circus performances given in our courts and in our senatorial investigations which . . . But we are in the Old Bailey.

The streets of London afford opportunities for a wide range of crime, and the police use a fine meshed net, leaving it to judges to assess the value — if I may use the word — of the crime. "Ten days or ten shillings," says my friend Sir Chartres Biron almost automatically at Bow Street Police Station. The problems presented to Sir Henry Dickens are more complex. Several hours were occupied with a case in which a pearl necklace of the value of four or five thousand pounds had disappeared. I think the necklace will reappear after a time, as Lloyd's, by whom it was insured, is deeply interested. Then there was an adjournment for luncheon, with a glass of port and an excellent cigar afterwards, and presently we are on the Bench again. Half a dozen petty cases are heard, sympathetically as it seems to me, and then there appears before his Worship an old man accused of " coining " — in other words, of making and circulating base sixpences, shillings, and half-crowns. Brief testimony is given.

"Are you innocent or guilty?" says Sir Henry.

"Guilty, your Worship."

"I seem to remember you. Have you been in this court before?"

"Yes, your Worship."

"What for?"

"Coining."

"How old are you?"

"Eighty-seven."

Whereupon Sir Henry, turning to a court clerk, says, "Have you this man's record?" It is produced, and Sir Henry glances at it and then, leaning over to me, says: "God bless my soul, look at this. The man is eighty-seven and has spent forty years in jail. He 's entitled to five years at the least, but I can't sentence a man of eighty-seven to five years." Turning to the prisoner: "You 're sorry for what you 've done, of course?"

"Yes, your Worship."

"And you 'd do it again to-morrow, if I let you go?"

"Yes, your Worship."

"I say you 'd do it again to-morrow, if I let you go?"

"Yes, your Worship."

"Don't stand there saying 'Yes, your Worship' to me. Is the man deaf?"

"Yes, your Worship."

(Louder.) "I say don't stand there saying 'Yes, your Worship' to me. Are you deaf?"

"No, your Worship."

"I 'm giving you a very light sentence in consideration of your age. When you come out of prison, where will you go — who will look after you?"

"No, your Worship."

(Louder.) "I say who will look after you?"

"My landlady, she will take care of me."

"Well, we 'll not let you give her any trouble for twelve months. Twelve months."

"No, your Worship."

"Don't stand there saying 'No, your Worship.' I say twelve months."

The prisoner is taken away; and, while the next is being called, Sir Henry says to me, "They were terribly severe in my father's day in sentencing criminals. At one time this old fellow would have been hung; later he would have been sent to Botany Bay." Upon which I suggested that his father had been the father of more reforms in England than all the professed reformers put together. And I thought how proud he would have been to see his son tempering justice with mercy.

A few weeks later, upon our leaving Paddington for Plymouth to take our steamer for New York, how reluctantly I need not say, Lady Dickens was at the station to see us off. They are dear old people, full of the courtesy of a generation — of two generations — ago. Sir Henry has now retired from the Bench. Before I left London I got Sir Henry to write in a copy of *Pickwick Papers* that he had found me an excellent judge, admirably fitted to preside at such a trial as Mr. Pickwick's.

It constitutes a sort of testimonial in the

event that my judicial experience is ever challenged.

The more I thought of my qualifications for a
judgeship, the more certain I became that a nice
snug berth upon the Bench was just the thing;
and so I got in touch with my friend, the Honorable William B. Linn of the Superior Court of
Pennsylvania, and asked him to reserve the next
vacancy for me. I told him of my qualifications and experience, and I think that I was making some headway with him when a brilliant idea
occurred to me. Why not secure a seat upon the
Supreme Court of the United States and make
a specialty of sentencing Senators and Con-
gressmen, making punishment fit their crimes?
As I read in the papers of the stupid, useless,
not to say criminal, wrangling in Congress in
regard to passing a tax law that would "bal-
ance the budget," as the saying goes, — the
country meanwhile bleeding, and not too slowly,
to death, — it came upon me with the force of a
blow: What good thing should I not deserve
from the country if I could send a crier out,
as they did in the good old days, and say to

Senator Loudmouth and Congressman Dolittle, "Come into the court and be hanged first and tried afterwards"?

I have in this little paper endeavored to express my contempt for the sort of government we have had in this country — what has been called "representative government." I cannot believe that we, as a people, are as contemptible as our "representatives" would lead one to suppose. For some years past there has been a steady deterioration in our public men. Fifty years ago there was, in our Senate, a group of men of which any nation might be proud. Their names were known to all; they were men of honor, ability, and training. To some extent this was also true of men in the House. But to-day this class, if it exists, finds itself practically unable to get into public life. Government, in the best sense of the word, has ceased to exist. We have laws enough, but they are not enforced. Our lawyers are corrupt and contemptible: it is from this class that our politicians are recruited and our judges selected. At present in this country neither life nor property is safe. Think of a nation of one hundred and twenty-five millions of people, with the accumulated wealth of several centuries, *with every bank closed!* Why? Because, for the most part, they were dishonestly administered. This was one of the accumulated results of one hundred and fifty years of democracy which came to an end with the cowardly impotence of Mr. Hoover. The incoming of Mr. Roosevelt, with his complete and courageous disregard for law and precedent, seems to have saved us from the anarchy and revolution into which we were steadily drifting. A new form of government has come into existence. I express no opinion of it; no one knows whither we are going, but we hope, if not for the best, at least for the better.

The country is too large, there are too many men in Congress, and it is too much in session. "They order this matter better in" — Egypt, where they have a constitutional King, Fuad. He takes his instructions from the English High Commissioner; but the Senators and Deputies got in his way, whereupon he thanked them very politely for their assistance and told them to go home and stay home until their services were required. Their pay was continued, so they made no complaint. I suggest that as soon as our Congress meets, its pay should stop.

If Mr. Roosevelt can find enough honest men to help him in our awful emergency, he may pull us out of our difficulties. But he will be wise not to look for such men in Washington. At this writing — July twentieth, 1933 — he is enjoying almost fatal popularity. There was a Roman Republic; it fell and was replaced by a Roman Empire; it, too, fell, but it was a long time a-falling. So it may be with us. History has a way of repeating itself, but always with a difference; so that it continues to be what Gibbon called it, "A register of the crimes, follies, and misfortunes of mankind."

P. S. — Dr. Johnson, in a letter to one of the Thrale children, written about a year before his death, says: "*Lily*, the white kitling, is now of full growth and very well behaved."

XVII

JOHN MYTTON

THE following little sketch of John Mytton is an extract from a paper on "English Color-Plate Books" that I read before the Print Club of Philadelphia about a year ago.

The event came about in this way: Two ladies, light-blue-stockinged women, in a manner of speaking, asked me to prepare and deliver this paper. They were charming women, or I would none of them; moreover, one was the wife of the Chief Justice of the Commonwealth of Pennsylvania, and the other the wife of a Superior Court judge. Now, in these days when traffic rules and regulations change every hour, one spends a good deal of his time before a chief justice, and, as the fines imposed by a chief justice are subject to review by a judge of the Superior Court, I thought it well to accede to their request. Everyone is aware that there are not enough lawyers to go round, and that it is almost

175

an impossibility to get a lawyer to go square; hence it is my invariable custom to throw myself on the mercy of the judge. At such times it is always well to have a friend at court— preferably two friends; hence this paper.

I am by nature a sedentary man, but color-plate books changed the whole course of my life. I have become a sportsman, an authority on horseflesh; I breed dogs and ride to hounds. I learned to swear, roundly, with Jack Mytton, — not difficult, — and to drink, deeply, with Jack Jorrocks, who claims, with some reason, that drinking will soon become a lost art. My friend Mr. Frank Raby was by my side when we stood with bowed heads at the grave of Mr. Mytton. "Take him for all in all, we shall not look upon his like again."

One of the most desirable of English sporting books is the first edition of *The Life of Mytton*. It is a small volume, originally published in 1835, and should be bound in brown cloth and contain twelve plates by Alken. Another edition appeared two years later, containing nine of the original twelve plates and nine new ones; and,

on account of the difficulty of obtaining the first
edition, booksellers frequently refer to the second
edition as most desirable because of the larger
number of plates — whereas the fact is that
the first edition, while almost unobtainable, is
greatly to be preferred.

John Mytton traced his family back for five
hundred years; so much for that. His father
died when he was a lad, and his mother's efforts
to keep him at school were unavailing; he was
expelled from Westminster and from Harrow,
and when at the age of fourteen, a ward in Chan-
cery, he appealed to Lord Eldon to increase his
allowance of eight hundred pounds per annum,
saying he was going to get married, that gentleman replied briefly: "Sir, if you cannot live on
your allowance, you may starve, and if you
marry I will commit you to prison." It would
have spoiled a very pretty biography had
Mytton not exercised every Englishman's right
to go to Hell his own way. With an iron constitution, Mytton entered upon a career of dis-
sipation, which ended only with his death from
delirium tremens in the King's Bench Prison in
his thirty-seventh year. He had by that time

succeeded in dissipating a fortune of ten thousand pounds a year and sixty thousand pounds in ready money which had accumulated during his minority.

Now, I don't mean to say that *The Life of Mytton* is a work of art or that it is my favorite biography, but I do say that if one wants to know in how many different ways a man can play the fool, it is essential to read this *Life*, and while doing so to remember that a hundred years ago Jack Mytton, Esq., M.P. for Shrewsbury, actually lived such a life as is presented by his biographer. The "strenuous life" that Mr. Teddy Roosevelt preached was the life of a valetudinarian compared with it.

But what did he do? you ask. We may suppose that the high spots in the life of this young barbarian, born without a nervous system, but with muscles of steel, are those chosen for illustration by Alken; and opening the book at random we come upon a man in a nightshirt with a gun in his hand squatting on the ice waiting for a covey of ducks to appear. This was not done on a bet; it appears that Mytton never felt either heat or cold, and that far from getting himself up in proper sporting togs, as men usually do when they go out, he, whenever the humor took him, went out in whatever he happened to have on; now he happened to have on a nightshirt when he felt a desire to shoot birds.

Another picture, showing two men being thrown out of a cart into the road, illustrates this story: Mytton was driving a friend home when he chanced to ask his friend whether he had ever been hurt by being thrown out of a gig. "No, thank God," was his friend's reply, "for I never was upset in one." "What!" exclaimed Mytton. "Never upset in a gig? What a damned slow fellow you must have been all your life!" And immediately he was running his offwheel up a bank; out they both went.

But the classical story, without which no reference to this book would be complete, is the one illustrated by the plate bearing the title, "Damn This Hiccup." The story may be briefly told. Mytton was in the act of getting into bed, when, annoyed by the hiccups, he exclaimed, "Damn this hiccup, I'll frighten it away," and, taking a lighted candle, applied it to his shirt tail and was instantly enveloped in

179

flames. When he was finally got to bed he stayed there for a considerable time.

How much he ate and drank, — from four to six bottles of port was his daily allowance, — the treatment of his wives, — he had two, — and many other details of this remarkable man were set down, not in sorrow, certainly not in anger, but in wonder, by his biographer; and we are quite prepared — as he was not — for his end. Ruined in estate, body, and mind, he fled to France; where, port being unobtainable, he lived on brandy. After a time he returned to England, where he was at once arrested for debt, the amount of which no one seemed to know. In a few weeks he was dead, and his remains deposited in all honor in the family vault under the Communion table of Halston Chapel.

"After life's fitful fever he sleeps well." Let us hope so.

XVIII

OLIVER GOLDSMITH

"SIR," said Dr. Johnson, "Oliver Goldsmith was a man who, whatever he wrote, did it better than any other man could do." This, indeed, is the sentiment which he subsequently translated into Latin for the famous epitaph in Westminster Abbey, and which, translated back into English, comes out as: "He left scarcely any style of writing untouched, and touched nothing that he did not adorn." I have always thought that, had Goldsmith chosen to add the autobiographical form of literary composition to the many which he so conspicuously adorned, he might perhaps have taken a thought out of the eccentric John Dunton's book and chosen for title "The Life and Frailties of Oliver Goldsmith." And should one, to-day, set one's self the delightful task of editing such a volume, one would, I am sure, set upon his title-page another of Dr. Johnson's well-known remarks: "Sir, let not his frailties be remembered; he was a very great man."

In all the realm of English literature there are few names greater than that of Oliver Goldsmith, and certainly there is not a man — unless it be Charles Lamb — of whom we think with more affection than the author of *The Deserted Village*, *The Vicar of Wakefield*, and *She Stoops to Conquer*. And when we think of the poet, the novelist, and the dramatist, we should also remember that he was a delightful essayist and biographer, and in some sense a historian. Well, indeed, might Johnson say, *Nullum quod tetigit non ornavit*.

One may be a confirmed Johnsonian and an ardent Boswellian — I am both — and yet be an excellent Goldsmithian too. One *may*, I say, but it would seem to be difficult: most men who delight in the great Lexicographer and his satellite seem to feel that Goldsmith's attainments and character are summed up in Garrick's silly couplet (I have it, in the actor's hand): —

Here lies Nolly Goldsmith, for shortness called Noll,
Who wrote like an angel, but talked like poor Poll.

OLIVER GOLDSMITH

The exigencies of rhyme are frequently responsible for a sad lack in sense. Now the fact is, "deny it who can," that, far from talking like poor Poll, the very best things in that best of all books, Boswell's *Life of Johnson*, were said by Oliver Goldsmith. Indeed, it would not be too much to say that neither Johnson nor Boswell fully appreciated him, and the reason is not far to seek. Johnson was English, Boswell was Scotch, and Goldsmith was Irish — in other words, he was a wit, and we seldom stop to think that the greatest English wits are invariably Irish, as will be seen upon reflection. What Johnson thought was vanity in Goldsmith, and Boswell conceit, was wit — wit too subtle for either the Englishman or the Scotchman to understand. Nations, like individuals, are merely animated prejudices; they do not seek to understand one another — they merely look down upon one another.

I am reminded of a story, new to me, and I hope it may be to my readers. An Englishman in Scotland went into a butcher shop and asked for a sheep's head. "Sandy," cried the butcher to his assistant in a back room, "bring me a sheep's head." "Mind you, an English sheep's head," explained the Englishman. "Sandy," cried the butcher, "take the brains out of it." Now, there you have it. Dr. Johnson's opinions of the Scotch are a matter of record, and to this day the English opinion of the Irish and the Irish opinion of the English are not fit to print. Yet on the subtle, delicate humorist, an Irishman, these two great men — for Johnson and Boswell are no less — did not hesitate to sit in judgment, and at times heavily.

But, notwithstanding all this, Johnson had the highest opinion of Goldsmith. If he "tossed and gored" him whenever he was present, he was unswerving in his admiration for his genius when he was absent. When the question arose as to who should write his (Johnson's) life, he said Goldsmith would do it best (this was enough seriously to disturb Boswell, who had already made up his mind to become his biographer); and when, in conversation, someone spoke slightingly of Goldsmith's literary style, Johnson immediately came to his defense with: "Is there a man now living who can pen an essay with such ease and elegance as he?" I never quite know what the critics mean when they use the word "nervous" to describe a man's literary style, but when I am told that a man writes with ease and elegance, I understand; and I can think of no one to whom these words more fully apply than they do to Oliver Goldsmith.

Have I overlabored the point? Perhaps I have, but my friend Mr. Elkins has asked me to write a few lines by way of introduction to the Catalogue of his famous Goldsmith Collection, and, glad to comply with his request, I had to say something. Mr. Elkins is fortunate in his selection of Mr. Temple. Scott to rewrite the well-known life and reappraise the well-known books. He has produced a very remarkable book, as anyone who turns its pages will immediately discover. Bibliographies are too frequently dull and unreadable; we pick them up to ascertain a fact or verify a point, and promptly put them down again. But this book is more than a bibliography: it is a biography as well, and the biography of a man whose very weaknesses endear him to us. And if it is not perhaps entirely complete as a bibliography, it contains a full description of the books in a

Goldsmith collection which is unexcelled, either in this country or abroad. Mr. Elkins's recent purchase of the so-called "Newbery Papers" has enabled Mr. Scott to clear up many interesting points about which we have heretofore been in the twilight — if not in the dark. The work, too, is given an additional interest by having for its frontispiece a little-known but obviously valuable portrait of Goldsmith, from the brush of Benjamin West, who, although he was born near Philadelphia, upon the death of Sir Joshua Reynolds was elected president of the Royal Academy.

I was lunching one day, some years ago, at the Cheshire Cheese with Walter George Bell, the eminent London antiquarian. "Is there anything particular in London that I can show you — anything that you have not already seen?" my host remarked. A wide choice was offered me. "Yes," I replied after a moment's pause, "I should like to see Oliver Goldsmith's chambers in the Temple, especially the room in which he died, described in your fascinating book, *More about Unknown London*." "That will be difficult, but not, I think, impossible," said Mr. Bell. "I know the present occupant, Mr. Hamilton Fox, very well. Let us look him up." At his office we were told that Mr. Fox was trying a case; a boy dispatched to find him and borrow the key presently returned with something resembling a small blunt battle-axe. With this implement in hand, we made our way to Brick Court — a London County Council plaque set high in the external wall marks the premises. We climbed the oaken stair, the treads of which had been worn into shallow troughs by the feet of many generations of occupants, unlocked the door, and entered with a feeling of reverence.

When Goldsmith moved into Brick Court in 1768, his affairs were, for him, flourishing, and he had purchased a life lease of the chambers. There were three rooms: one an amply proportioned sitting room with three large windows overlooking Essex Court; a smaller room, which tradition says is the room in which he wrote, overlooking Brick Court; and a tiny interior chamber, hardly more than a large closet, with two doors and no window — and it was in this room that the great man died. It is now full to overflowing with books, as indeed Goldy would have had it; and it is crowded with memories.

It is what one feels rather than sees that is the joy of such a visit as ours. Familiarity with the details of Goldsmith's life, and Johnson's and Boswell's and Garrick's, helps enormously. Does my reader remember that Blackstone lived in the chambers just under Goldsmith's, and was frequently disturbed in his legal studies by the high jinks of Goldy and his friends? This anecdote of Blackstone is all the law I know (I know lawyers who know less). And I remembered the little girl who came to the door to borrow a chamber pot full of coals for her mother — and got them, too. I thought of the dying poet and recalled the insistence with which to the last he took Dr. James's Powders, — the then fashionable remedy (Horace Walpole said he would take them if the house were on fire), — and of the remark of Dr. Turton, his physician, "Is your mind at ease?" and of the patient's melancholy reply, "No, it is not": these were his last words. He died on the fourth of April 1774, having lived forty-five years and five months.

It was midnight, a few days later, when down the stairs a small group of men carried the coffin and, reaching the ground, raised it to their shoulders and trudged with it to a grave which had been dug a little distance north of the Temple Church. The interment would have taken place in the Abbey but for the poet's debts: it was feared by his friends that an effort might be made to seize the body. We wonder whether Mr. Filby, Goldy's tailor, who lived hard by in Water Lane, would have lent his countenance to anything so disgraceful. Had he not furnished the poet with his bloom-colored breeches, his name would long since have been forgotten. Who would not gladly exchange a pair of un-mentionables for immortality? "Was ever poet so trusted before?" exclaimed Dr. Johnson, when he heard that his friend's debts amounted to two thousand pounds. The idea pleased him: to be able to owe two thousand pounds was the next best thing to having it.

Goldsmith's grave was unmarked for years; it was not, indeed, until 1856 that a stone was placed, and by that time the exact site of inter-ment had been lost — but what difference does it make? Somewhere, in the shadow or in the sun, — it now matters not, — near the stone on which is the inscription, "Here lies Oliver Goldsmith," his mortal part was buried; but his immortal part, his writings, — so easy, so elegant, so witty, — these remain to tell us what manner of man he was, and for these we love him, as has been said of a greater man, "this side idolatry."

XIX

AUTOGRAPHS

THERE are more plums and less batter in this book[1] than in any other book on this subject that I know of. And on a shelf not far from the table on which I write I see a row of *Rambles* and *Meditations* and *Diversions* and *Talks* and *Chats* — and a lot besides — about Autographs, but Lady Charnwood has written a better book than any of them. Nor is this my opinion only. In a book catalogue which drifted to my desk only yesterday from James F. Drake of New York City I read this: —

AUTOGRAPHS. Charnwood (Lady). An Autograph Collection and the Making of It. Illustrated with facsimiles. 8vo, boards, half cloth. London, 1930. $5.00. First edition. By all odds the best book on the subject, written from the standpoint of a collector.

[1] *An Autograph Collection and the Making of It,* by Lady Charnwood, Henry Holt & Co.

So there you have it: my opinion confirmed by one who knows.

Lady Charnwood writes on her subject with a verve which the average Englishman tries to conceal; but then, Lady Charnwood is neither "average" nor, as we should say, one hundred per cent English. She has a dash of Italian blood in her of which she is very proud; she had a grandfather whose name was Mundella. He became a naturalized Englishman and a member of Parliament, and a bust of the old gentleman from the chisel of Sir Edgar Boehm stands in her drawing-room. This is not, however, the important thing. An inscription informs us that its "cost was defrayed by 80,000 factory workers, chiefly women and children, in grateful acknowledgment of what he had done for them."

But to return to the Lady and her Hobby. She has a large collection of autograph letters and many of them are excellent, but other collections are as good. The merit of her book consists in its wise saws and modern instances — *e.g.*, "Match up your letters yourself and save money" (the phrasing is mine, but the

192

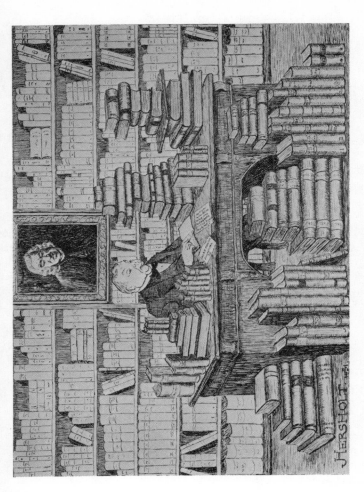

A. E. N. Is Asked to Autograph a Book

A caricature by Jean Hersholt

idea is the Lady's); "The best way is to purchase from one dealer, and that an expensive
one"; "Luxuries always command their value
. . . the glorification of the best at the expense
of the second best is certainly the fashion of the
moment"; "It is well to have a record of the
place, price, and date of buying; it makes a
most interesting history."

It will be seen that the Lady has "views" and
expresses them with neatness and dispatch.
When they agree with mine, — and they usually
do, — she is right. She knew Gladstone and
loved him; I did not know him and I never
admired him. Of Gibbon's *Decline and Fall*
she says, "I have read it from cover to cover
and can honestly say that I wish it were longer."
I do not wish it longer, and Sam Johnson felt
that way about *Paradise Lost*. I am in entire
agreement with her about Gibbon's Autobiography. "It is one of the best ever written
and it should be better known." It is these
obiter dicta which make Lady Charnwood's
book so delightful. She knew Henry James,
who called her his dear child, and Burne-Jones,
and Millais, who painted her portrait, and

Browning, who, when she was a child, said to her, "The greatest surprise of my life was when I went to see my wife one day before our marriage and she got up to receive me. I was engaged to her before I knew that she could stand."

On the subject of the arrangement and the indexes of an autograph collection she has "views" which she says are extremely strong. They are; she knows what she knows and — quite as important — what she does not know, but she knows where to find out about it, which is the next best thing. She says she knows little of "paper" and is "extremely anxious" about forgeries, but I feel quite certain that the Englishman now residing in Paris who, with the help of a notorious London bookseller, is flooding the market with forgeries of Shelley, Byron, Stevenson, Brontë, and other authors found the Lady "not at home" to his wares.

Lady Charnwood's book, autobiographical as such a book must be, is especially so in the last chapter, where she describes her country mansion, "Stowe House," near Lichfield. It was, a hundred and fifty years ago, the home of the Reverend Mr. Gastrel, who with his wife was a friend of Dr. Johnson, who frequently visited there; subsequently it was the home of Thomas Day, the author of *Sandford and Merton*. In it he sought to train the two young girls, one of them to be his bride, the other to be satisfied with the gift of a marriage portion, and the right to look for a husband elsewhere — which, in the event, both young girls did. Thomas Day is perhaps best known for his remark, "A lawyer is more noxious to most people than a spider."

XX

CHARLES DICKENS

IN the winter of 1931, John Galsworthy gave a lecture in Philadelphia on the English Novel. I did not hear him; I am much too wise: I lecture myself occasionally, but I never go to lectures. I consider it a waste of time, as you will, too, when you have listened to what I have to say.

But Galsworthy is reported to have said that the greatest English novelist was Charles Dickens, with which I agree, and then he went on to say that his favorite novelists were Stevenson, Katherine Mansfield (of whom I have, knowingly, never read a line), Conrad (whom I can't read at all), W. H. Hudson, and Mark Twain. He added that Margaret Kennedy's *The Constant Nymph* would outlive most of the books of this generation, and closed his lecture by saying that Mark Twain's *Tom Sawyer*, Hawthorne's *The Scarlet Letter*, and Norris's

McTeague were the three outstanding things in literature that this country has produced.

Good! I like a man who is not afraid to prophesy. I have read *The Constant Nymph*, enjoyed it at the time, and have now forgotten it completely. I should have said *Huckleberry Finn* rather than *Tom Sawyer*. I agree about *The Scarlet Letter*, and I think *McTeague* — well, it can hardly be too much praised. But where is *Moby Dick*, or *The Whale*, as they call it in England? This is our one great contribution to literature. But, as I have said elsewhere, it is a difference of opinion that makes stock markets and horse races interesting, and the same may be said of novels.

I put Dickens next to Shakespeare as a great genius, though, like Shakespeare, he is very uneven; but we should think of Dickens as Steerforth wished to be thought of, "at his best." He has conferred the greatest blessing upon the English-speaking world that it is in the power of man to bestow — namely, that of amusing us; or, to state the same fact in other words, of making us forget our own real troubles in the troubles of the creatures of his imagination. I may

197

remind you that it was Swift who observed that "whoever could make two ears of corn to grow where only one grew before would do more essential service to his country than the whole race of politicians put together"; and Laurence Sterne, who was, in a way, a forerunner of Dickens, took the same thought and said that he who could make a man smile, still more when he could make him laugh, deserved well of mankind. It is not now our habit to laugh loud — the loud laugh bespeaks the vacant mind, as Goldsmith has it; rather are we, by the genius of Dickens, lifted out of a world of care, of anxiety, of pain even, into another in which we entirely forget ourselves. This is the joy of reading.

Our idea of pleasure changes: as children we enjoyed what, being grown up, bores us unconscionably. In like manner, we can no longer tolerate what our grandfathers called pathos. Some ninety years ago Walter Savage Landor (savage by nature as well as name), a man of sixty-five, wrote to Forster that Dickens "has drawn from me more tears and smiles than are remaining to me for all the rest of the world, real or ideal." It is almost beyond the power of the novelist to-day to move the world to tears. The death of Paul Dombey, that impossible child, with his "What are the wild waves saying?" leaves us cold, and we no longer "fall for" Little Nell, who, as some critic has said, is "a Hollywood angel-child." We see a high eccentric, man or woman, going down the street, and we tell each other, "There is a character right out of Dickens." This phrase, so applied, has passed into our language, but we don't mean exactly what we say; what we mean is that the person referred to has the characteristics — rather, the idiosyncrasies — of some individual immortalized by the genius of the Master. Let us think of Pecksniff or Wilkins Micawber, or Mrs. Jellyby. Dickens did not create characters so much as he did attributes which he endowed with life. As this may be regarded as a serious charge, I may be permitted to labor the point for a moment.

Mr. E. M. Forster, a distinguished English critic, in a recent study of the English novel says we may divide characters in fiction into flat and round. Flat characters in their purest form are constructed not so much of flesh and blood as of a single idea or quality; when they get an increasing number of ideas or qualities they tend to become round. A really flat character can be described in one sentence so many times repeated that we forget that the repeater of it is flat. There is Mrs. Micawber: she lives in a phrase. She says "she will never desert Mr. Micawber." She never does, and there she is. The last we see of her she is clinging to the arm of her lord and master on the deck of the boat as it swings out into the river. She said she would never desert Mr. Micawber; she never has, and we know that she never will. Miss Betsey Trotwood is by no means flat, but she has her flat moments when she chases donkeys with the help of her servant Janet. Mr. Dick, with his King Charles head and his kite, is very flat. But Sir Leicester Dedlock is not flat, nor is his Lady; nor Jonas Chuzzlewit nor Mr. Wackford Squeers; and certainly Mr. Dombey and Sydney Carton are not. And when, in 1870, the famous chair at Gadshill was made empty by death, that death did, in very deed, as Dr. Johnson said of David Garrick, "eclipse the gayety of nations and impoverish the public stock of harmless pleasure."

It is not curious that there has grown up about Dickens an immense — shall I call it literature? Most of it is of indifferent quality; some of it is very bad indeed. I need not remind you that Dickens at the age of twenty-six enjoyed such popularity as no other author ever had before — or since. He rose like a rocket and he has not yet come down, and we Dickensians feel that he never will; but in his upward flight he carried with him, inevitably, a host of lesser men. And almost before his body was cold in the Abbey every one of these men rushed into print with a book. And Charles Dickens is presented to us, not indeed as a flat character, but as a very round one, round as a ball is round and of immense size: so large that we cannot grasp it, and opaque so that we cannot see through it, and we are forced to see one facet only — if a ball may be said to have a facet — at a time. So we have Dickens as a novelist, and Dickens and the law and lawyers, and Dickens and the stage, and Dickens as an actor and an editor and a lover, husband, father, friend, and as this, that, and t'other thing. This being exhausted, we have Dickens in London and in Bath and in Boston — here, there, and everywhere; but the real Charles Dickens, the man whose life was so carefully secreted by his wise and official biographer, Forster, in three large volumes, is only now coming to light. The two best books about Charles Dickens are the volumes by Gissing and by Chesterton. To these I should, perhaps, add *The Man Charles Dickens*, a psychographic study by Edward Wagenknecht of the University of Washington, on the Pacific Coast.

In matters of taste we must not judge Dickens by the standards of our own time. In his day it was not a crime to be a fop, to wear one's hair long, sticky with Macassar oil and highly perfumed, with noisy clothes (perhaps I should say nothing about this). It was not a crime in his day to drink much wine, to challenge public attention by an exuberance of spirits. Think of another novelist, Disraeli, later to become Prime Minister of England, wearing clothes which shrieked to heaven, with violet kid gloves, and rings on them, not beneath them. "The apparel oft proclaims the man," but not always:

the times have much to do with it. And times have changed not alone in the matter of clothes; they have changed as much, or more, in the expression of one's emotions. We read much, as I have said, of tears in Dickens's day. Dickens wrote with the tears streaming down his face, — or said that he did, — and what he wrote had the same tearful effect upon his readers. Stony-hearted judges accustomed to send men and women to the gallows, or the hulks, wept copiously at scenes which now bore us so exquisitely that we skip them and, for good measure, much else. But in his own time he was read for those very qualities which we should willingly see absent from the most enduring of his works.

What, then, remains? Much. Scholars are largely agreed that the greatest creation of Shakespeare is not Hamlet or Lear or Macbeth, but Falstaff. There is profound wisdom in the remark of Horace Walpole: "Now I hold a perfect comedy to be the perfection of human composition, and I firmly believe that fifty *Iliads* could be created sooner than another such character as Falstaff." *Sic itur ad astra* (in Latin),

"Thus to the stars" (in English), might well have been the motto unconsciously adopted by Charles Dickens when he sat down to write, properly speaking, novels which placed him among the greatest creative geniuses of the world. He ranks with Cervantes as a humorist. He has, I verily believe, given more intellectual pleasure to more people than any man that ever lived. Of great tragic writers, as of great tragic moments, the world has, it may be said, enough and more than enough. When Messrs. Chapman and Hall sent for an obscure journalist, only twenty-four years of age, and invited him to write the text to certain sketches of Robert Seymour, the illustrator, who could have supposed that they were assisting at the birth of a character who may — nay, almost certainly will — last as long as the language itself? And not Mr. Samuel Pickwick only, for, as someone has felicitously pointed out, in the fifth number, as Beatrice would say, "a star danced and under it Sam Weller was born." Don Quixote and Sancho Panza, Mr. Pickwick and Sam Weller — these two couples will go hand in hand down the ages.

CHARLES DICKENS

An orator once said that the sun never sets in the Spanish dominions. This was much too fine a phrase to be confined to Spain. Daniel Webster took the thought, gave it a twist, and, in a speech of great magnificence, applied it to British possessions. Can it not with equal truth be said of the *Pickwick Papers?* Somewhere now, at the moment, wherever the English language is spoken or read, or a translation therefrom has penetrated, someone is reading this great book for the first, or the fifth, or the fifteenth time.

And not *Pickwick* only, but many of the books of the great immortal. One book appeals to one man, another to another. My own choice, with some notable exceptions, is the last that I have read. The first editors of Shakespeare said that he had never blotted a line. Ben Jonson, in reply, wished that he had blotted a thousand; and the same may be said of Dickens. I could wish the whole first chapter of *Martin Chuzzlewit* blotted. It is the worst first chapter of any great book ever written, as, in my opinion, the first chapter of *Great Expectations* is the best. I once knew it almost by heart. "My father's name being Pirrip and my Christian name

Philip, my infant tongue could make of both names nothing longer or more explicit than Pip. So I called myself Pip, and came to be called Pip." Then follows that wonderful scene with the convict in the churchyard near the tombstone of Georgiana, Wife of the Above, and other magnificent bits follow one after another. And you remember the scene where Pip tells Joe Gargery that Miss Havisham, far from having four dogs that fought for veal cutlets out of silver baskets, had n't even a puppy. I hope Joe Gargery is one of your favorite characters; he is one of mine.

I have suggested — indeed, I have done more: I have insisted that *A Christmas Carol* is the greatest little book ever written, and I am not in the least downcast by the statement of a professor of literature that he finds it "grossly sentimental and grossly overcharged with violent conversions of the Christmas Spirit." Good! May I try to prove the correctness of my opinion by pointing out how much more charity and humanity and loving-kindness there is in the world to-day than there was before the *Carol* was first sung that Christmas Day in the year

1843, and if Charles Dickens did not teach these virtues, who did? I ask you. Certainly no preacher of any denomination whatsoever. "Business," cries the Ghost, wringing its hands, "mankind is my business. The common welfare is my business; charity, mercy, forbearance and benevolence are, all, my business. The dealings of the trade are but a drop of water in the comprehensive ocean of my business." There is the Christmas Spirit! — and the spirit of Charles Dickens.

I have referred unsympathetically to the death of Paul Dombey; I could talk in like manner of the death of Little Nell, but to what purpose? The only bit of melodrama that I can tolerate is the death of Jo in *Bleak House*. "Dead, your Majesty. Dead, my lords and gentlemen. Dead, Right Reverends and Wrong Reverends of every order. Dead, men and women with Heavenly compassion in your hearts. And dying thus around us every day." But I prefer to think of Mr. Pumblechook, the farinaceous corn-chandler, Mr. Chadband with his large yellow smile, and Mr. Pecksniff and his interesting daughters, Charity and Mercy; of Peggotty and Steerforth, and Mrs. Gamp, who did not care to be asked "whether I won't take none, or whether I will," but who wished the bottle placed on the chimney piece that she might put her lips to it "when so dispoged"; and of her friend Mrs. Harris, of whom I may say with confidence that no artist was great enough to limn her.   But I have said enough, perhaps more than enough, of Charles Dickens; the world is divided, unequally, into those who idolize him and those who do not.   I am one of those who do; it is not often that I find myself thinking with the majority.

XXI

CAROLYN WELLS AND HER BOOKS

HERE in the midst of this awful heat comes a request — a command, rather — from Carolyn Wells that I write a brief introduction to the Sale Catalogue of a portion of her library. "Dear A. Edward," she says, "you must write a few lines and send 'em to Mitchell Kennerley for my catalogue; you got me into this mess, it 's up to you to get me out. When this letter reaches you I shall be on the briny."

What am I to do? I can't "wireless" the lady where to go; she is probably ill by this time and thinks she is there already. I know what she means by the "mess." Several years ago we were in my library and I was showing her with pride a small blunder in a book which greatly enhanced its value. "And this mistake by that stupid printer adds eighty dollars to the value of that book?" she inquired.

"It does," I replied.

"Well, I call this game the Idiot's Delight," was her rejoinder.

"All right," I said, "you qualify."

"Tell me where to begin," she said.

It's great fun to bandy words with Carolyn Wells, but when she decides to do a thing she does it with an amount of intelligence that might lead you to believe that she is exhausting herself; but not so — she is only drawing upon her surplus energy. Now I believed at the time, and I still do, that anyone who wants to get the greatest sport out of collecting rare books cannot do better than to buy "Americana," for, whatever happens to democracy (and I am the last man that would wish to save it), I believe that the continent is safe.

That reminds me of a story. I have a friend in San Francisco; he is a stockbroker on a large scale, and an old lady came into his shop, wanting to make an investment. Van Antwerp — that's the broker's name — is very conservative, and would not commit himself as to the value of some gilt-edge securities she considered buying. Finally she said, "Well, then, it's your opinion that I should buy Government bonds; you regard them as absolutely safe, I suppose." "Well," said Van, cautiously, "I would hardly say that; but they will be among the last things to go."

Now, next to bonds on the continent, I believe in books about it. (I have n't any myself, and don't want any, for the reason that they don't interest me; my passion is English literature.)

"What do you fancy?" I inquired of Carolyn.

"Something American," she said.

"In that case," I replied, "you could not do better than Walt Whitman. As a singer — God, no! not as a singer, but as a yelper — of the brotherhood of man, he is destined to take an important place."

"Comics are more in my line," said she; "but I believe you are right. I 'll take on Whitman."

And the next thing I knew people were telling me about Carolyn Wells's Whitman collection; and after a year or two I heard that she had the finest lot of Whitman that had ever been put together. Then someone told me that she was doing a bibliography, and I asked her about it.

"Bibliography, no," she said; "check list, yes. Great fun."

Then I heard that her Whitman collection was to be sold; then I heard that it was n't. Then, that she was selling some rare duplicates and some other choice items because she had gone off on another tangent. It may be so, I do not know; very likely it is. But in whatever direction she has gone, people will know that she has passed that way.

Coming back to Whitman. I firmly believe that the first edition of *Leaves of Grass* will reach a higher figure than any other important book published in the nineteenth century — and I do not forget that valuable Shelleys and Keatses were published in that century. I may not be around at the time. If I am not, let some kindly disposed soul go west, "change cars at Paoli," take a motor, and visit the Washington Memorial Chapel at Valley Forge (that 's where these "Democratic Vistas" start), and, after visiting the Chapel, which is one of the loveliest shrines in America, search out my modest tombstone in the leaves of grass near by, sit down upon it, and whisper to me, "You were right about that Whitman item." I shall be listening eagerly for the latest prices of rare books.

XXII

WILD ANIMALS IN THE LIBRARY

THAT a middle-aged book-collector — who can call only the domestic animals by name with any degree of certainty, whose knowledge of trees is limited, and whose ignorance of flowers is unlimited; who has no sense of smell, and to whom the twittering of all birds is alike — should enjoy *Wild Folk* [1] speaks volumes either for the dawning of his intelligence or for the charm of the book itself.

When this book was sent me to review I said, as many another reviewer has said under similar circumstances, "I shall review this book, but I shall not read it." Then, upon turning its pages, I said, still to myself, "I shall read this book, but I shall not review it" — for the reason that it is not my kind of book; there is nothing in it about Dr. Johnson, or the eighteenth century, or any-

[1] *Wild Folk*, by Samuel Scoville, Jr., the Atlantic Monthly Press.

thing else that I have any knowledge of. I get my pleasure indoors, whereas the author of this book gets his happiness in the open.

But, after all, it is my kind of book: any book is my kind of book that I can read with delight. Mind, I cannot vouch for the truth of any one of the ten stories contained therein; but I am not asked to. When one reads a novel one is satisfied if the story gives pleasure and if it *might* be true. These stories are quite as interesting as though they were written about people: to the author wild folk are people — that is quite evident.

You, reader, may know that canvasback ducks can travel at the rate of one hundred and sixty feet per second; but I did not. I suppose that ducks, like men, are known by the company they keep, and I have usually seen canvasbacks in pretty fast company, especially in cafés in New York. But one hundred and sixty feet per second is going some! However, canvasbacks do it with ease, Sam says. Elsewhere he talks about birds being "anchored" in the sky. Now I maintain that's a very pretty bit of writing, and the book is full of such.

WILD ANIMALS IN THE LIBRARY

I suspect the author of having appropriated Joe Hergesheimer's palette, or whatever he gets his color words from. He uses them very freely, as one is careless with a stolen automobile. Sam has no time for ordinary colors, such as ladies' silk stockings come in. He paints in turquoise and sapphire and amethyst and silver and gold and copper and steel and rose-red and lavender-brown and carmine-lake and gamboge-green and heliotrope. Joe flings color about as though it cost nothing; evidently Sam has taken a leaf out of his book, and I don't know that he could have done better.

Birds and animals and snakes and bugs interest Sam amazingly. He would find intelligence in June bugs, which I had always supposed had no intellect whatever. When they throw themselves on their backs and wave their feet about in the air, they have a reason for so doing, and it is up to us to discover whether their reason is good or no before we criticize them.

And the skunk. Sam says that maybe the Boche learned the secret of gas attack from this animal. He describes a brief encounter between a small skunk and a large fox, after which only one thought remained in the fox's mind, namely, air; air, fresh untainted air, preferably miles away; and he departed to find it.

If any father can read the story of the Coon Family without being a better father for the experience, I am sorry for him. And children should read this story and learn obedience to parents, which is all too rapidly going out of fashion — at least it is in my family. Among wild folk disobedience means death, and he who makes one mistake never gets a chance to make another.

While I was reading *Wild Folk* I had occasion to go to my dentist, and a thought occurred to me: is it for our sins that our teeth are so defective? The meanest animal that grows seems to have better tooth equipment than we humans have. I must ask Sam why this is; he will know.

I wonder whether there is any truth in the story he tells of a man who, when a Liberty Loan drive was on, bought a bond for himself and another for his dog — who wore, and seemingly with pride, a Liberty Loan button in his collar. I don't think Sam has enough imagination to make this up ; he is a very close observer, and must have seen it somewhere.

Wild Folk is a nice book to own, and to read, and to give away.   But I never give a book away — 'less it 's poetry.

INDEX

INDEX

Byron, Lord, quoted on Burton's *Anatomy*, 99, 100

CAMPION, EDWIN B., death, 47; funeral, 47, 55, 56; anecdotes of, 48–54
"Captains of Industry," 161
Carlyle, Thomas, 33
Caxton Head, 139, 142–144
Cervantes, Miguel, 204
Charles I, King, 69
Charnwood, Lady, her *Autograph Collection and the Making of It, An*, 191–195
Chesterton, G. K., his *Charles Dickens*, 202
Christmas cards, 127–129
Christmas Carol, A, published in 1843, 124; and the Christmas spirit, 124, 125, 206, 207; original manuscript of, 126; presentation copies of, 126; Dickens's copy of, 126; first copy of (a "pull" from the type), 126, 127; and the Christmas card, 128; the greatest little book ever written, 206
Christmas Day, 121, 123
Christmas spirit, 121–129, 206, 207
Christmas trees, 124
Cleveland, William H., his book collection, 31, 32
Coleridge, Samuel T., "The Ancient Mariner," 19; compared with Lamb, 23, 24
Collins, Wilkie, his *The Moonstone*, 89
Color-plate books, 174, 175
Congress, the American, 172, 173
Congreve, William, his *Incognita*, 27; his *Robinson Crusoe*, 90
Conrad, Joseph, 196
Cowper, William, 68
Croker, John Wilson, 86
Cross, Wilbur L., his *The Life and Times of Laurence Sterne*, 104–110; his *The History of Henry Fielding*, 104; his *The Development of the English Novel*, 104

Cunningham, Alison, Stevenson's nurse, 146
Currie, Barton, 76
Cushing, Dr. Harvey, 100

DAVIS, EVELINE BELWOOD, marries James Tregaskis, 141
Day, Thomas, his *Sandford and Merton*, 195
Defoe, Daniel, *Robinson Crusoe*, 86–94
Dell, Floyd, 98
Dickens, Charles, 27; *Martin Chuzzlewit*, 7, 8, 205, 207, 208; on Lamb's "Dream-Children," 10; Birrell's love for, 25; *Pickwick Papers*, 26, 170, 114, 115, 204, 205; and Seymour, 114, 204; creation of Pickwick, 114, 115; *A Christmas Carol*, 124–128, 206; reforms brought about by, 170; his rating as a novelist, 196, 197, 204; great blessing bestowed upon mankind by, 197; his humor, 197, 198, 204; Landor on, 198; pathos in, 198, 199, 203; his eccentric characters, 199, 200; created living attributes, 199; flat and round characters of, 199, 200; the literature about, 201, 202; his popularity, 201; *Great Expectations*, 205–207; *Bleak House*, 207
Dickens, Sir Henry Fielding, 165–170
Dickens, Lady, 170
Disraeli, Benjamin, 202
Drake, Sir Francis, 62
Drake, James F., 191
"Dream-Children," original manuscript of, 5, 9, 24; charm of, 8, 11; last paragraph of, 8, 24; written on India House paper, 9, 24; first title of, 9, 10; Canon Ainger on, 10; Lucas on, 10; Winchester on, 11; original publication of, 11
Drinker, Henry S., Jr., 76

INDEX

Dunton, John, 181

"EDITION," the term, 87, 94
Elizabeth, Queen, 69
Elkins, Mr., his Goldsmith Collection, 185, 186
Emmanuel, Victor, 20
England, 62; New Forest, 64; Portsmouth, 64–69, 71; Bucklers Hard, 64; Greenwich (Wren Chapel), 69, 70
English, and Scotch, 183, 184
Escott, T. H. S., his book on Trollope, 74
European Bookbinding Exhibition, 1891, 140
Evans, A. W., 137
Evelyn, John, 122
Everyman's Library, 32

Fanny's First Play, 40
Filby, Mr., Goldsmith's tailor, 189
Forster, E. M., his study of the English novel, 199
Forster, John, 198; his *Life of Dickens*, 202
Fox, Hamilton, 187
Franklin, Benjamin, 28
Fuad, King, 173
Fundamentalism, 64

GALSWORTHY, JOHN, on the English Novel, 196
Garrick, David, 188, 200; his couplet on Goldsmith, 182
Gastrel, Rev. Mr., 194
Genius, 78
Gibbon, Edward, 112, 174; his *Decline and Fall*, 193; his Autobiography, 193
Gilbert, W. S., quoted, 58, 61
Gissing, George, his *Charles Dickens*, 202
Gladstone, W. E., 193
Goldsmith, Oliver, and Johnson, 181–184; the variety of his productions, 181, 182; and Boswell, 182, 183; the ease and elegance of his style, 184, 185; West portrait of, 186; his

chambers in the Temple, 186–188; his death, 188; his burial, 189; his debts, 189; his grave, 189, 190; on the loud laugh, 198
Goldsmith Collection, Mr. Elkins's, Catalogue of, 185, 186
Gray, Thomas, his *Elegy*, 27
Greene, Belle da Costa, 106, 126

HAMILTON, LADY, 67
Hardy, Capt., of the *Victory*, 66, 67
Hardy, Thomas, 71; *Under the Greenwood Tree*, 39
Harmsworth, Sir Leicester, 26
Hawthorne, Nathaniel, his *The Scarlet Letter*, 196
Heathcot's Intelligence, 90, 91 n.
Henry VIII, King, 69
Hergesheimer, Joe, 215
Hind, Lewis, 33
Hoover, Herbert C., 130, 161, 173
Hudson, W. H., 196
Humor, invaluable in a novelist, 79
Hutchins, Henry Clinton, his *Robinson Crusoe and Its Printing*, 86–88, 90, 93, 94

INTERNATIONAL Bindings Exhibition, 1894, 140
Irving, Washington, his *Sketch Book*, 127
"Issue," the term, 87, 94

JACKSON, HOLBROOK, 102; his *Anatomy of Bibliomania*, 40, 97; his *The Eighteen Nineties*, 97, 98; his edition of Burton's *Anatomy*, 98
James I, King, 69
James, Henry, 193
Jeffrey, Lord, 125
Johnson, Charles Plumptre, Dickens collector, his *Hints to Dickens Collectors*, 126
Johnson, Dr. Samuel, 68, 99, 133, 213; editions of, 25; his definition of a lexicographer, 88; remark of, on Burton's *Anatomy*, 95; on test of literary merit,

INDEX

INDEX

224

INDEX

DATE DUE

DEMCO 38-297